110630

DATE DUE			

Court Reform

Ideal or Illusion?

Steven W. Hays
California State University

Lexington Books
D.C. Heath and Company
Lexington, Massachusetts
Toronto

Library of Congress Cataloging in Publication Data

Hays, Steven W.
  Court reform.

  Includes bibliographical references and index.
  1. Courts—Florida. 2. Courts—United States. I. Title.
KFF508.H38   347'.759'01   77-10348
ISBN 0-669-01841-4

Copyright © 1978 by D.C. Heath and Company.

Published simultaneously in Canada.

Printed in the United States of America.

International Standard Book Number: 0-669-01841-4

Library of Congress Catalog Card Number: 77-10348

to Anne Marie, Angela, and Alison

Contents

List of Figures

List of Tables

Acknowledgments

As is true with any work of this nature, I have incurred many debts. I am especially indebted to Larry C. Berkson and William Kelso for reading and analyzing the manuscript. Their efforts contributed greatly to the clarity and consistency of usage in the text. I am also indebted to Manning Dauer and Ernest R. Bartley who not only gave me the benefits of their wisdom regarding the Florida political culture, but also read the manuscript and offered valuable suggestions for revisions.

I would like to thank the many court clerks, judges, court administrators, and other judicial personnel whose comments comprise the most interesting and useful part of this work. In addition, the Staff of the Joint Select Committee on Judicial Personnel, the Florida Supreme Court, and the Office of the State Courts Administrator contributed data, documents, and other information that was essential to the completion of the manuscript. Finally, a special acknowledgment is due my wife, Anne Marie, whose assistance and support is greatly appreciated.

Each of these people improved the quality of this work greatly. None, however, bears any responsibility for errors, omissions, or inaccuracies that may have resulted. Any deficiencies in this work are, of course, my own responsibility.

Court Reform

1 Introduction

The Problem

State judicial systems have traditionally been composed of numerous semi-autonomous courts.[1] This phenomenon may be attributed both to the federalist system and to an American affinity for what is termed "local responses to local problems." Thus, county and state governments have been allowed to create and manage their courts according to local standards, regardless of the macro-justice system. The practical effect has been the establishment of a profusion of specialized courts with overlapping and inconsistent jurisdictions. Individual courts normally function as distinct administrative units without any semblance of centralized direction or supervision.[2]

The fragmentation and decentralization that have characterized state trial courts are considered to be largely responsible for the persistence of archaic judicial management techniques. Because local governments are primarily responsible for providing financial and personnel resources to the judicial systems, the vagaries of county politics influence the level and quality of court support services. At best, this arrangement has resulted in procedural and administrative inconsistencies among courts in different counties and states. At worst, the capabilities of many courts to perform their functions adequately has been seriously hampered. Some state court systems employ a plethora of outmoded and seemingly inefficient procedural and administrative practices. Partially as a consequence of these archaic management techniques, the courts have been increasingly incapable of meeting the demands imposed by rapidly expanding case loads.[3] Such dilemmas as court delay and inequitable applications of the law serve to illustrate the significance of judicial inefficiency.[4]

In response to the growing crisis in the courts, a vast array of reforms have been suggested by both legal and academic scholars. The bulk of these recommendations propose that state judicial systems be "centralized" and/or "unified" in order to bring administrative rationality to the courts.[5] By unifying state court systems under a centralized administrative authority, proponents anticipate that fragmentation will decline and administrative anarchy will be replaced by continuity in procedures, thus facilitating court modernization.[6] The establishment of consistent rules, procedures, and levels of managerial competence is viewed as being essential to the very survival of our system of justice. According to David Saari, ". . . a court with impaired management produces an inferior brand of justice."[7] If this assertion is valid, then irregulari-

1

ties in the structure jeopardize the legitimacy of both the courts and the political system as a whole.

The Pursuit of Reform

The legal community has long been active in court reform. Roscoe Pound's 1906 address to the American Bar Association signaled the beginning of the reform movement in America.[8] Pound criticized court multiplicity, concurrent jurisdictions, and the resulting waste of judicial manpower. These condemnations logically resulted in reform proposals that were grounded in the concepts of unified courts and administrative simplicity.

Although Pound's indictment of the courts was not originally well-received by the legal profession, by 1938 the ABA had adopted many of his proposals in its resolutions for judicial reform. The resolutions, known as the Parker-Vanderbilt Standards, were designed to begin the process of establishing the judiciary as an *independent* branch of government. They called for unified judicial organization, full rule-making authority vested in the courts, and the utilization of administrative judges.[9] These reform suggestions were expanded by the 1962 ABA Model State Judicial Article.[10] In addition to calling for simplified structure and clear lines of administrative authority, the Model Article included pleas for merit selection of judges, the appointment of professional court administrators, and judicial discipline and removal mechanisms.

The latest and most sophisticated reform proposals emanating from the legal community were issued in 1974. The ABA *Standards Relating to Court Organization* incorporate almost all of the conventional wisdom of Pound and his successors.[11] The *Standards*, however, depart from most earlier reform positions in regard to at least one major structural component.[12] Whereas previous reform groups advocated a two-tier trial court—one of general and one of limited original jurisdiction—the recent *Standards* support the utilization of only one trial court. Proponents of this structure contend that a one-level court will result in more efficient use of judicial resources. According to one analysis, simplified jurisdictional divisions, more uniform standards of justice, and clearly vested policy-making and administrative authority will also result from the elimination of limited jurisdiction trial courts.[13]

Despite minor disagreements among reformers over the exact structural composition of the "ideal" court system,[14] there is virtual unanimity regarding the major tenets of reform. Unification, simplification, and clear lines of administrative authority and responsibility have become articles of faith among most students of court modernization. These concepts have gained wide currency and are presently the fundamental components of the court reforms that have been instituted in past decades.

While members of the legal profession have been diligently and successfully pursuing reform for over fifty years, social scientists have been relatively inactive. Primarily as a result of the "upper court myth,"[15] trial courts have been virtually ignored by political scientists and sociologists. Only recently has the political and social significance of lower courts been recognized. Prompted by frequent reports of "unequal justice" and court delay, scholars are broadening their areas of inquiry to include all levels of the justice system. For example, several authors have recently analyzed the administration of local justice in order to ascertain the effects of various procedural practices on the quality of justice dispensed.[16] The political influence of trial courts has also become a major area of research.[17]

Although the increasing tendency of social scientists to examine trial courts is pronounced and significant, academicians have traditionally failed to investigate the specific area of court management.[18] The managerial dilemmas of judicial organizations have been largely overlooked. The literature of public administration concentrates almost solely on the other branches of government.[19] The disinclination of social scientists and public administrators to scrutinize court administration may be attributed to the fact that court systems are bureaucratic enigmas. This conceptualization is predicated on several factors. First, court systems depend upon the cooperation of numerous actors who are not employees of the judiciary. Second, judges are "professionals" and thus are motivated by normative, not administrative, values. Finally, participants in the judicial process exhibit numerous conflicting goals and behaviors that cannot and should not be subjected to administrative "routinization."[20]

Nevertheless, academic attention to judicial management problems is currently on the increase. As a result of advocacy from such sources as the ABA and Chief Justice Warren Burger to name a few, court systems throughout the nation have employed court administrators. Court management is evolving into a profession that requires new knowledge to maintain itself. To meet this need, several textbooks that examine the administrative vagaries of the courts have recently appeared.[21] The reports of numerous study commissions on dilemmas in the criminal justice system have provided a further impetus for increased research. Current maladies in judicial administration are thus beginning to be addressed by an expanding cadre of academics and practitioners. To state that the total body of knowledge regarding court-related operations and administration has tripled in the past five years would not be an exaggeration.

However, several fundamental omissions exist in the literature that has been generated by the sudden interest in court management. Most authors concentrate upon such general operational and "process" aspects as jury management, space utilization, procedural causes of delay, and judicial selection and tenure techniques. Few studies of judicial administration acknowledge the existence of any group of actors other than judges and attorneys. Consequently, the total organizational context of judicial activities has been largely ignored. In order to comprehend fully the intricacies and exigencies of court reform, judicial structure must be viewed in the total environmental setting. The crucial elements of this environment include quasi-judicial support structures, the formal and informal interactions between these structures and judicial personnel, and the external political variables that dictate the nature of such interactions. The support structures, as defined by this study, are staffed by such personnel as court clerks, deputy clerks, and court executive assistants, or court administrators. These aspects of court management constitute the least studied and consequently the least understood facets of judicial administration.

Although the importance of support structures and other external factors has not been totally recognized, a few authors have briefly noted the potential influence that quasi-judicial officers may exert on judicial activity. For example, James A. Gazell states that court clerks and court administrators, by virtue of their strategic administrative position, may become "staff competitors for judicial leadership" nominally exercised by chief judges.[22] Because these personnel possess expertise, they may gain de facto control of state judicial bureaucracies. Chief judges may be experiencing what their counterparts in other bureaucracies have encountered: a widening gulf between authority and expertise.[23] Court operations, and the directions that reform movements take, may thus be primarily determined not by judges but by their support personnel.

The ability of court clerks to resist the power of judges has also been documented. For example, Jerome Berg questions the rationality of placing major administrative control in the hands of independently elected and appointed officers. He concludes that no argument in favor of independent clerks compensates for the necessity ". . . of giving those who are responsible for the efficient administration of the courts the requisite control of the entire organization."[24] As independent officers, clerks have historically presented judges with a multitude of management problems involving office management procedures and clerical techniques. The fact that elected court clerks do generate management dilemmas for the courts has been verified in several studies, with the latest being a 1977 examination of Illinois circuit court clerks.[25] Unfortunately, the last detailed analysis of this situation was published in 1947.[26]

The fact that most state courts rely upon locally oriented support structures has also been cited as one of the primary reasons for the fragmentation and decentralization of trial courts. The judiciary is tied by these support structures to "local and partisan values that encourage haphazard administration."[27] The consequence of such a system has been a lack of central direction, planning, and active management among court organizations. The view that local orientation leads to irregularities in the management of trial courts thus suggests that the level and quality of justice available to the citizens is affected.

The level of political influence enjoyed by the personnel who occupy quasi-judicial positions has also been investigated. Richard Gable's account of court reform in Los Angeles County indicates that administrative personnel can marshall a rather large amount of political support to resist reforms that threaten their bureaucratic position.[28] In light of this fact, the suggestion that the support personnel, as a collectivity, represent a formidable power in state politics assumes added significance.

The literature thus reveals that certain aspects of judicial organization exist that have not traditionally been evaluated in terms of their impact on court administration. Although the administrative influence of support structures has been assumed for some time, the consequences and dimensions of this influence are poorly understood. The necessity of comprehending all factors that might affect the nature of judicial administration generally, and court reform specifically, cannot be underestimated. As reform movements accelerate throughout the nation, consideration of these factors represents a particularly timely issue.

The Progress of State Court Reform

Reform of state court systems is progressing at an ever-increasing pace. The most noteworthy aspect of the reform movement is the degree to which most judicial revisions are in accordance with the proposals of Roscoe Pound and the ABA *Standards.* "Unification" and "reform" are regarded by most authorities as being synonymous. The major components of the unification movement are the following: consolidation and simplification of trial and appellate court structures; centralized rule-making authority vested in the chief justice and/or the supreme court of the state; administrative responsibility vested in a central office, usually through a system of trial and state court administrators who are administratively subservient to the judiciary; and a system of state financing of all court expenses.[29] Although few states have implemented these reforms in their entirety, most states are currently adopting portions of this traditional depiction of a unified system.

The two reform components that appear most frequently are consolidation of trial courts and centralized rule making. The trend toward simplification of trial court structure is especially pronounced. Although there is a general lack of consensus over the optimal number of trial and appellate courts in a unified system, the fact that the number of trial court tiers is declining nationwide is regarded as the crucial factor for the purpose of this study.

Presently at least thirty-five states have taken steps to simplify their lower court structures. Such reforms vary from the elimination of special courts to the establishment of the ultimate in unification, a one-tier trial court of general jurisdiction. The trend toward lower court unification is so prevalent that James A. Gazell predicts that by the mid-1980s all states will implement some type of simplified structure.[30] During the 1976 general elections, ballot issues that included the consolidation of trial court organization were approved in Missouri and North Dakota.[31] Since that time the state of Wisconsin has followed suit.[32] Current developments thus indicate that Gazell's prognostication may well be too conservative.

Centralized rule making is a similarly popular development. Prior to the reform movement most states allowed the legislative branch to control the rule making authority of the judiciary. However, this situation is rapidly changing. Reform groups are nearly unanimous in advocating that the judiciary be allowed to control its own procedures and rules without active legislative involvement. This argument is predicated on the belief that only through centralized rule making will the courts develop uniform, consistent, and "workable" procedures. To date, thirty-two states vest this authority exclusively in their supreme courts.[33] An alternate method of providing centralized rule-making authority is to allow judicial councils to perform these functions. Only California and New York currently employ the council form. The remaining states divide rule-making authority among a combination of entities, including the judiciary, state legislatures, and judicial councils.[34] Most court unification measures that are currently being considered vest rule-making authority entirely in the state supreme court.

In addition to centralized rule-making power, most reformers agree that a truly unified court system must have a clearly defined locus of administrative authority. Such an arrangement is deemed essential for the efficient development and implementation of reformed policies and procedures. Centralized administrative authority is also viewed by most reformers as a prerequisite to the implementation of court supervised planning, personnel, budgetary, judicial assignment, and records-keeping systems.

As with trial court consolidation and centralized rule making, the pace of court reform in this area has seemingly been rapid. Whereas specific lines of administrative authority and accountability were essentially nonexistent in state court systems just twenty-five years ago, a majority of states now apparently function according to a traditional organizational framework. The chief justice of these states is normally designated the administrative head of the system. Presiding judges in each individual county or regional court depend upon the chief justice for administrative direction. Assisting these persons is a cadre of professional court administrators who are responsible for the day-to-day management of the judicial organization. While this is the "ideal" depiction of an administratively centralized court system, a recent comparative study of court unification movements implies that most courts fail to operate in such a manner.[35] Although the centralized administrative mechanism exists in a purely organizational context, extensive authority is not being fully exercised in many instances. Thus, reform in the area of centralized administration is lagging behind other aspects of judicial "modernization."

A similar phenomenon is apparent in regard to the last major component of court unification. Despite the fact that state financing of all or most judicial expenses is perceived as a central tenet of court unification, Carl Baar's landmark study indicates that most states are hesitant to adopt this reform. According to Baar, in the six-year period between 1968 and 1974 the overall proportion of judicial activities funded by state governments increased only 2.3 percent.[36] Although this figure will indubitably be revised as a result of such post-1974 reforms as those in Alabama[37] and Kentucky,[38] the slow increase is extremely significant. State court funding is regarded by most reform groups as the most direct method of expediting the institution of other types of judicial reform. Thus, the disinclination of state governments to implement centralized funding indicates that the commonly accepted depiction of a unified court is not receiving total endorsement.

Despite the noble objectives of court reform, progress in bringing a *pure* form of unification to state court systems has been slow. This fact is hardly surprising. The effects of two centuries of fragmentation and decentralization cannot be expected to evaporate rapidly in response to a legislative or constitutional dictate. There exists in every state a number of factors that affect the ability of reformers to institute needed change. Unfortunately, very little is known about many aspects of state court management that exert a great deal of influence upon reform attempts.

The present endeavor to examine these factors essentially constitutes a case study of the systemic reform of a large state court system. The relative success of court reform movements has traditionally been measured in terms of the quantity of professional court administrators hired, the number of constitutions revised, and the degree to which the court structures relate to reform commission proposals. Although these factors are indeed noteworthy, they do not reflect the entire truth. The best possible constitutional revision of a court system is of little utility unless it results in the intended substantive administrative changes. Examination of the experiences in one state, as in this case study, serves to illustrate the obstacles that confront reformers.

This study examines three variables that are most critical in evaluating the potential success of reform attempts: the personnel responsible for administering the courts; the traditional management practices utilized by these personnel; and the political and institutional context in which their duties are carried out. The study is an organizational one that explores the relationship between the traditional modes of operation and the espoused desires of reformers. The examination can be broken down into subareas of research questions that are explored in some detail, including the following:

1. What impact has decentralization had on the system of justice under study? How do these factors affect the efficiency of the court?
2. How do the roles, attitudes, and perceptions of the court administrators influence the acceptance of change? Which of these factors are particularly relevant to court management?
3. What proposals can be offered to help eliminate the traditional inefficiencies of the courts? Which of these will also be useful in overcoming obstacles to reform?

4. What political and cognitive realities exist that may obviate reform attempts?

The Florida Experience

The data required to operationalize this study was primarily compiled on the twenty circuit courts and sixty-seven county clerks' offices that together comprise the bulk of the judicial administrative machinery in the state of Florida. The four district courts of appeal were not included in the analysis due to their comparatively minor role in the total administrative composition of the system. Each of Florida's sixty-seven counties also contains a county court. The chief judge of each circuit court is constitutionally responsible for the "administrative supervision of the county courts in his jurisdiction."[39] Consequently, the administration of the county courts was examined only insofar as it related to the activities of the personnel in the circuit court and county clerks' offices.

The court system of Florida offers a particularly fruitful opportunity to study the interactions between court personnel and their environment. There is substantial evidence that, according to the conventional theories of court reform, the Florida court system is one of the most progressive and advanced judicial structures in the nation. On March 14, 1972, the voters of Florida approved the revision of Article V of the state constitution, which essentially resulted in the complete restructuring of the statewide court system into what is widely assumed to be a unified whole. Former Chief Justice B.K. Roberts characterized the passage of Article V when he stated: "In one sweeping move to modernization, uniformity and consolidation, overwhelming voter approval was given to a new court system which has already been heralded as one of the most modern in the nation."[40]

The immediate effects of the adoption of Article V somewhat resemble the most optimistic desires of many judicial reformers. The basic provisions of the amended article created a unified state court system that consists of the Florida Supreme Court, four district courts of appeal, twenty circuit courts, and sixty-seven county courts (table 1-1). The supreme court and the district courts of appeal were relatively unchanged in the new system, while the lower courts were radically altered. All trial level jurisdiction was vested in the circuit and county courts. Jurisdiction of the two courts was defined uniformly throughout the state, with the circuit courts having general jurisdiction and the lower courts limited jurisdiction.[41] All county judges' courts, county courts, civil, criminal and felony courts of record, small claims' courts, juvenile courts, and justices of the peace were abolished and replaced by the two-tier court structure. This change resulted in a consolidated court that is reportedly "... uniform in jurisdiction, geographically divided, and which has clearly defined administrative and jurisdictional authority."[42]

These radical alterations were not accomplished without some degree of difficulty. The Florida Constitutional Revision Commission, which was responsible for preparing a revised version of the Florida Constitution for action of the 1967 legislature, presented that body with a proposal that was deemed unacceptable. The legislature diligently attempted to arrive at a settlement as to the content of the article, but too many conflicting ideas were presented. Subsequently, a new Article V was proposed by the legislature and was placed on the ballot in the 1970 general election. This proposal was defeated by the citizens of the state. That election had been preceded by a vigorous campaign on the part of those both favoring and opposing the amendment, and its defeat left Article V as the only section of the 1885 Florida Constitution still in effect.[43] Another revision was then drafted by the Florida House and Senate Judiciary Committees after hearings were held around the state and preliminary drafts were circulated for comments and suggestions.[44] This last version was submitted as an emergency matter to the voters on the March presidential preference ballot. It was approved this time by a two-to-one margin. Most commentators attribute the radical change in public opinion to a successful voter education program sponsored by the proponents of Article V. Moreover, court delay was becoming more common and more visible, thereby providing them with a tangible campaign issue.

The history of the adoption of Article V serves to illustrate the politically sensitive nature of court reform. It is typical of struggles that have occurred repeatedly within the past ten years. It also furnishes valuable insights into the problems and conflicts that have been confronted by reformers in other states. The structure of Florida's court system prior to the adoption of Article V greatly resembled the judicial structure and administrative machinery that presently exists in many areas of the United States. Moreover, the revised structure incorporates many of the most significant components of a unified system. In addition to consolidation of trial courts, the Florida judiciary enjoys centralized rule-making authority and a centralized administrative structure. The only major aspect of the "ideal" unified court that is lacking is the absence of extensive state funding. This general framework closely parallels the administrative composition of courts in a vast majority of "reformed" and transitional court systems.

Perhaps of even greater significance is the rather typical nature of Florida's judicial environment. Florida is a large state; yet it is clearly separated into both rural and metropolitan geographical areas. Moreover, court clerks are independently elected officers and control much of the court administrative machinery in the state. Similar conditions exist in at least thirty-five other states.[45] Finally, the initial reactions to reform that were displayed by many judges and clerks in Florida have already been repeated in numerous other reform movements, including those in Georgia,[46] Michigan,[47] and Kentucky.[48] As a consequence, Florida provides an excellent "laboratory" to examine the process of reform.

Table 1-1
Florida Court System before and after Article V

Level	Before Article V	After Article V
I State-Wide	Supreme court, seven justices, six-year terms, elected.	Supreme court, seven justices, six-year terms. No change in structure.
II District Courts of Appeal	Four courts of three judges each, six-year terms, elected.	Number of districts and number of judges to be determined by general law enacted by the legislature on recommendation from the state supreme court. Judges are elected for six-year terms. General law may provide for special divisions.[a]
III Circuit Court	Twenty judicial circuits, one judge for each 50,000 people. No specialization by judges on particular cases.	Any number of judicial circuits as recommended by the supreme court and as determined by general law. Circuit judges to be elected for six-year terms. General law may provide for a system of special divisions. The circuit courts have appellate jurisdiction from lower courts and original jurisdiction over cases not falling to county courts. Probate jurisdiction is assigned to the circuit courts.

IV County and Local Courts

A. County court or county judges in each of 67 counties. Counties could also have special courts such as civil court of record, criminal court of record, juvenile court.

B. Justice of peace courts, courts in counties not having abolished them by law.

C. Municipal courts as established by law.

A county court with one or more judges is established in each county. Jurisdiction and possible special divisions are established by general law. Judges shall serve for four-year terms, be paid by the state, and while existing judges even if not lawyers may be eligible to run? thereafter, only lawyers may serve except in counties with less than 40,000 population. Jurisdiction supersedes magistrate courts. Justices of peace were discontinued when this article became effective, and municipal courts were abolished as of January 3, 1977.

Source: Manning J. Dauer, "Amendment Revising Florida Court Structure," Civic Information Series, No. 52 (Gainesville: Public Administration Clearing Service, 1972), pp. 4-5. Reprinted with permission.
[a]The election of appellate judges was eliminated by a 1976 constitutional amendment.

The events surrounding attempts to implement the article can be expected to reflect occurrences that may surface as other states attempt to implement similar reforms. The predispositions and characteristics of the personnel intricately involved in implementing reform in Florida are assumed to be quite similar to those of their colleagues in other states. Finally, the traditional management procedures and techniques that have yet to be replaced in Florida are largely representative of practices in most other states. The budgeting and personnel systems utilized by Florida's court clerks are representative of those employed throughout the nation, as are numerous other facets of their organizational makeup. Thus, the problems, inefficiencies, and conflicts present in Florida's experience with reform have wide applicability and should enlighten future reformers as to the obstacles they confront.

Courts as Organizations

The study of courts as complex organizations has been popularized within the past several years. Thus, this study also endeavors to analyze court structures as they relate to contemporary organization theory. According to one view, court systems encompass the key elements of complex organization: ". . . institutionalized interaction of a large number of actors whose roles are defined, who are required to follow explicit rules, and who share common goals."[49]

Such a depiction of the judicial system is somewhat iconoclastic. Because courts are not highly centralized and structured organizations, theorists have traditionally treated them as nonbureaucratic entities. The virtual absence of formal control mechanisms also contributed to the perception of courts as informal, not formal, organizations.[50] Most organizational theorists assumed the judicial system was intentionally designed to avoid the routinization endemic to complex organizations so that adversarial proceedings would not assume the complexion of bureaucratic "process." Although the merits of this argument are obvious, few scholars now question the validity of the conception of courts as organizations.

Viewing courts as simply another group of government bureaucracies provides several advantages not found in more traditional treatments of such institutions. An organizational analysis expands the legitimate areas of inquiry. Typical concerns of researchers examining government agencies include: (1) the interrelationships between the formal and informal systems; (2) the nature of the values, roles, and individual goals exhibited by organizational members; (3) the nature of the organization's environment; (4) the level and complexity of the technology employed to attain specific goals; and (5) the number and types of organizational goals. Each of these factors is pertinent to an analysis of court organization and the effects of reform on that organization.

The formal system is commonly defined as the rational set of rules and structures that prescribe behavior within an organization. Conversely, the informal system consists of the spontaneous components such as values, prejudices, and unprescribed social structures that evolve whenever humans interact. Although behavior within organizations is shaped by a variety of factors, the relationships between these two systems are influential in determining the nature of organizational activity. Courts, due to their decentralized and relatively unformalized structures, are especially susceptible to the influences of the interactions between the systems. The introduction of innovative reforms into the judicial structure is likely to upset the delicate balance that has existed between these systems for a century or more. The probability exists that reforms, which by definition redefine the nature of organizational interaction, will encounter opposition from the informal system. Role conflict, "bruised pride," and other forms of friction-invoking situations can be expected to arise. Each administrator's role conceptions, attitudes, and individual goals will thus exert an influence upon the level of acceptance and success that reform achieves.[51]

The fact that organizations are strongly influenced by their environments is widely recognized. The link between judicial systems and their environments is particularly profound. Due to the traditional conception of courts as neutral governmental organs, the judiciary has been hesitant to assume an advocacy role in obtaining increased appropriations, personnel, space, and equipment.[52] This practice has resulted in a bureaucracy that is extremely dependent upon external political bodies. Courts are also unique in that they do not possess a viable clientele group through which to seek external support. Other important elements of the environment of judicial systems include: the support structures and suppliers that are not formally involved in the administration of the court, including legislative bodies, states' attorney's offices, diversion centers, probation and parole commissions, and sheriff's offices; and the competitors of the organization, which consist of other government agencies competing for resources.

The conceptualization of courts as organizations is predicated on the assumption that judicial systems have finite goals. However, a major obstacle confronting students of court organizations is that there is a lack of clarity concerning the nature of the formal goals of the judicial bureaucracy.[53] On an abstract level, court administration is normally considered to be directed toward the achievement of "justice." Justice is a function of procedure, due process, and the equally abstract concept of fairness. Efficiency, the announced goal of reformers, is often viewed by the legal community as being antithetical to the formal organizational objective. Efficiency and administration supposedly connote an abandonment of due process considerations to financial and temporal exigencies.

The concern of legal theorists with this depiction of the courts can be attributed to what Etzioni terms "the goal model of organizations," in which the criteria for measuring the effectiveness of any organization is based upon the announced public goals of the administrative unit being studied.[54] If the goal of the bureaucracy is assumed to be justice, then the level of organizational efficiency is determined by ascertaining the degree to which justice is produced. However, such a conceptualization is impractical because the concept of justice cannot be empirically tested. Moreover, analysts following the goal model tend to become preoccupied with formal structures and thereby ignore other important variables.

As a result, this study utilizes a more open-ended conceptualization of judicial goals. First suggested by Malcolm Feeley, the "systems model" of organizational activity is applied to the courts.[55] This approach provides two major advantages over the goal model. First, a realistic appraisal of the internal interactions of judicial organizations is facilitated, thus enabling the researcher to isolate specific problem areas. Second, the courts are portrayed as being multifunctional units, thereby expanding the scope of the study to include nongoal oriented activities such as administrative operations.

The major difference between the two models is that the courts are viewed as being composed of a large number of persons with different and often conflicting objectives.[56] Each member of the court system possesses a unique set of values, perceptions, and backgrounds. Thus, a perfect coincidence of organizational goals with the informal goals of judicial actors cannot be expected. A pronounced discrepancy between these two types of goals (individual and organizational) will eventually elicit conflicts that will quite probably appear in an interpersonal or institutional context. The presence of conflict often denotes the existence of dysfunctional activities or attitudes that affect the ability of the organization to adjust to its environment. Consequently, unless mechanisms are developed to secure compliance to the formal goals, internal dissention could conceivably inhibit the attainment of organizational efficiency and institutionalized reform.

The importance of examining the nongoal-oriented aspects of judicial organizations is related to the courts' systemic goal of justice. In the American judicial system, the process used to reach a specific decision is as important as the nature of the decision itself. "Justice acquires meaning in a normative and legal context only when operationalized in terms of procedure."[57] Responsibility for most of the procedural aspects of jurisprudence has now been arrogated to the support structures in response to the increasing amount of litigation. Therefore, if inefficiencies exist in the service and maintenance organs of a court, the litigants' chances of receiving a fair hearing are reduced. Justice is an elusive goal in a court that employs ineffective procedures or that lacks adequate resources to perform its functions.[58]

While efficiency and effectiveness are the goal of most court reformers, a debate is currently germinating in regard to the appropriate *means* for achieving those ends. Specifically, some disagreement over the composition of the optimum form of court administrative structure has developed. As has been discussed, the traditional wisdom of court reform prescribes a unified system with clearly vested lines of authority and accountability. This ideal is to be accomplished through centralized rule making and administrative authority, state financing, and a centrally administered personnel system.

Critics of the traditional definition of reform draw their inspiration from contingency theory. This school of organizational theory contends that management structure and operations should be contingent upon a number of variables, including the level of environmental stability, technological complexity, the nature of the work force, the timing of activity, and the size of the organization. Adherents to this school liken centralization, unification, and consolidation to Frederick Taylor's "principles of management"—guidelines that assert that only one correct way to manage exists.[59]

David Saari and Geoff Gallas, two of the forerunners in the application of contingency theory to court reform, argue that the traditional wisdom encourages overcentralization and rigidification of court operations.[60] According to contingency theory, centralization is not an optimum response to management dilemmas in an organization that is staffed by professionals, that has a complex and uncertain technology, that has little control over its inputs, and that is extremely interdependent with other organizations in the environment.[61] The unique nature of judicial organizations requires a strategy different from that advocated in the reform literature. The peculiar nature of each court should first be analyzed before administrative reforms are operationalized. Moreover, the specific reforms that are implemented should vary according to both the local situation and existing structures. Generally theorists of this school conclude that flexibility, decentralization, and responsiveness to local needs are appropriate conditions that should be maintained and encouraged.

The debate over the relative advantages and disadvantages of centralization furnishes valuable insight into the motives and responses of court personnel in transitional judicial systems. Demands for flexibility and decentralization on the part of judges in Massachusetts have already led to the successful implementation of a relatively "modernized" system that is primarily decentralized.[62] If, as the Massachusetts experience indicates, unification is occasionally an inappropriate response to judicial maladies, the reform experience should indeed be a lively one.

Methodology

The information used to compile the analysis of the Florida court system was obtained from three primary sources: (1) semistructured personal interviews with a number of judges, court executive assistants, and court clerks in the state; (2) questionnaires distributed to these persons; and (3) various documents composed by agencies and commissions concerned with court reform in Florida. In addition, participant observation data was used to supplement and verify several of the conclusions reached.

The three groups of personnel studied comprise the bulk of personnel responsible for court administration in Florida. These groups include the chief judges of the twenty circuit courts, the seventeen court executive assistants employed by the circuits, and the sixty-seven court clerks. The chief justice of the Florida Supreme Court and the Office of State Courts Administrator are also posts of considerable importance to judicial management in the state. While the administrator and members of his staff were personally interviewed, information from the office of the chief justice was obtained primarily from policy statements emanating from the supreme court.

A total of twenty-eight in-depth interviews were conducted during a seven-month period. Although representatives from all three major groups of administrators were interviewed, only data concerning chief judges was collected exclusively through this technique. It was assumed that personal contact with these persons would enhance the quality of information received. In two cases individual judges were interviewed over the telephone due to scheduling difficulties.

The interviews followed the form outlined by Claire Sellitz et al., in which questions are structured in such a way as to allow respondents a degree of freedom in their replies, and the instrument was flexible enough to allow concentration on particularly useful topics or to abandon unprofitable lines of questioning.[63] Organizational goals, budgeting dilemmas, constitutional inadequacies, administrative inefficiencies, judicial philosophy, and a number of other topics were discussed. Among the major issues explored in detail were: (1) the background variables of respondents; (2) attitudes concerning other personnel in the judicial system; (3) conceptions of court reform and the court system generally; and (4) administrative matters relating to leadership, communication flow, organizational structure, and informal relationships. Of particular interest to the interviewer were the responses of the three judges (this number has now been reduced to two) whose circuits do not employ court administrators. Comparisons were made between those circuits that seemed to exhibit an active interest in reforming judicial administration and those that appeared less concerned.

Data concerning the court executive assistants and court clerks was obtained through the use of questionnaires. Of a universe consisting of seventeen court executive assistants and sixty-seven court clerks, 82.3 percent ($N = 14$) and 86.6 percent ($N = 57$) responded, respectively. This high return rate was unexpected inasmuch as the research instrument was of a relatively lengthy nature. Moreover, many of the court personnel who had been contacted during the design of the questionnaire had expressed chagrin and open hostility toward the increasing amount of forms, questionnaires, and "red tape" that accompanied the implementation of Article V. This fact dictated the omission of several questions that were perceived to be relevant but that would have increased the size of the questionnaire to a prohibitive level.

Research techniques developed by Herbert Jacob,[64] Angus Campbell,[65] John Robinson and others[66] were incorporated into the questionnaire. A mixture of open-ended and fixed alternative questions were employed.[67] The instrument was designed to gather data falling into three major categories: (1) that dealing with personal characteristics, background variables, and pre-entry training; (2) that dealing with attitudes toward, and interpersonal relationships with, other individuals within the judicial system; and (3) that concerning the administrative design and operation of the court structure. The data provided insights into administrative problem areas, attitudes toward reform, the level of professionalism present in the circuits and a variety of other issues. Variables such as the size of the respondents' counties, their levels of education and pre-entry training, and their conceptions of official duties were held constant in order to identify possible relationships. Finally, attitudes concerning roles, functions, and duties were juxtaposed against the legally defined position descriptions.

Cross-tabulations were utilized to determine the relationships between a number of variables. This technique proved to be particularly fruitful because the responses of all administrators within many circuits were obtained. Thus, if a particular administrator's replies revealed any unusual or unexpected relationships, those pieces of data could generally be verified by cross-tabulating them with the responses of the person's colleagues. Moreover, information relating to the perceived roles and duties of each administrator could be evaluated more effectively by examining how the other personnel in the system viewed him.

Information supplied by the staff of the Joint Select Committee on Judicial Personnel proved to be exceptionally useful. The researcher had originally intended to distribute questionnaires to a sample of the four thousand deputy clerks in the state. However, repeated efforts to contact these personnel were frustrated by the court clerks. Consequently, information relating to training methods, technological complexity, and internal office management was lacking. Much of the missing data was supplied by the committee, as well as a sizable amount of information regarding the political and managerial intricacies of the Florida judicial system. Among the items furnished by the committee were statistical surveys concerning the organizational size and structure of many local court systems and numerous suggestions for systemic reform. Moreover, the staff's access to legislative and supreme court policy proposals enabled a more comprehensive analysis of the macro-political environment of the judicial system than would otherwise have been possible.

During the course of this investigation, ample opportunity was available to observe the various administrators in their "natural" environment. The knowledge and insights gained through these observations have been incorporated throughout this study. Observation assisted the researcher in developing more substantive questions and provided a deeper understanding of the temper of the organization. However, any conclusions contained in the present analysis that are based entirely upon such observations are clearly noted as such.

2

The Florida Court Structure
and Personnel

A History of the System

Before the implementation of Article V the Florida judicial system lacked centralized administrative direction and a locus of responsibility. This deficiency resulted in a fragmented and unmanageable structure. Each court formulated its own administrative rules and procedures. Salary levels for judges were so inconsistent that often judges in the most responsible positions were paid far less than their colleagues in minor courts. Individual administrators and judges determined the personnel requirements of their particular courts. No one person was responsible for collecting statistics to determine the financial and judicial requirements of the various court systems. No single person had the authority to transfer judges between jurisdictions, to discipline trial judges, to establish uniform procedures, or to pursue any activity requiring the coordination of the various elements of the system.

This anarchistic situation was aggravated by the tendency to create specialized courts to meet the exigencies of a rapidly changing society. As was common in most states, the response to judicial backlogs brought about by increasing amounts of automobile, civil, and juvenile litigation was to simply create new courts to administer these neoteric areas of the law.[1] This approach was dictated, in part, because legislative alteration of the judicial system is much simpler to accomplish than is constitutional revision. The general assumption was that special courts could be created to meet present needs and then be abolished.[2]

Political considerations also explain the popularity of creating special courts. Legislators discovered that such courts constituted a vehicle for dispensing political patronage. While the legislators were able to create political offices for their party supporters, the constituents of each district viewed the special courts as justified legislative responses to local judicial requirements. Despite the abundant political advantages offered by this "solution" to court reform, the state legislature was not obligated to appropriate funds to establish the special courts. Since the individual counties financed the court system almost entirely, legislators would seldom object to the creation of the new courts in districts other than their own.[3]

Consequently, special courts became judicial appendages in every county in Florida. For example, in 1970 sixty-three variations of court names and jurisdictions were estimated to exist within Florida's counties.[4] These courts became separate entities, which thus created new sets of vested interests. The county clerks and judges exercised concurrent control over the courts situated in their locales. Judges and clerks "controlled" the administrative aspects of their courts with little or no intrusion from central authorities. The amount of appropriations allocated to each court often depended upon the political relationships between the court managers and local political bodies. Because the clerical functions were the responsibility of the independently elected clerks, and not directly under the control of the courts, altercations between the court managers themselves were not uncommon. The situation that existed was somewhat analogous to a judicial feudal system in which each court represented a separate feifdom where responsibility and control were divided between several factions.[5]

The negative consequences of this decentralized system of justice were myriad. Due to the extensive number of judicial structures, overlapping and inconsistent jurisdictions were common. Potential litigants were confronted by a profusion of courts that conceivably had jurisdiction over their cases. Because the courts were dependent upon local political bodies for financial support, great disparities in levels of funding existed. Courts located in wealthy communities, or in areas where the court's relationship to local political authorities was especially salutory, could generally provide a better level of services to their clients than courts located in less advantageous environments. Due to the lack of organized personnel systems, judicial employees were often hired on a patronage basis and were thus dependent upon the judge or clerk for tenure. The fact that the court clerks dictated the terms of employment resulted in gross disparities between counties in salaries, fringe benefits, and qualifications of personnel. Attorneys practicing in courts located in different areas were often confronted by dissimilar procedural requirements and legal forms.[6]

Perhaps the most serious consequence of the fragmented court system resulted from the internal administrative practices of the court clerks and judges. Because the clerks' offices have traditionally been the primary administrative arm of the courts, an alienated clerk was in an ideal position to subvert the operations of the judiciary. The clerks' strategic role as administrator over clerical procedures, space, and equipment in the counties was supplemented by his dual role as chief budgetary officer. Consequently, the judges were often required to maintain positive working relationships with the clerks in order simply to insure continued financial and operational supports.[7] This phenomenon further complicated the status of court administration in the state, for responsibility and accountability could never be established as long as the judicial organizations were serving two masters.[8]

The systemic and structural disorganization that existed in Florida's courts provided the impetus for the reform movement that culminated in the passage of Article V of the Florida Constitution. As has been previously stated, Article V reorganized the Florida court system into a consolidated structure with fixed

21

administrative responsibility. With the exception of municipal courts, which were not abolished until January 1, 1977, all special courts were abolished and uniformity in jurisdiction was instituted (figure 2-1). The supreme court was empowered to certify to the legislature the need for additional lower court judges. The judicial power of the state was vested in four levels of courts, and the policy-making and rule-making authority for the supervision of the judicial branch was delegated to the supreme court.[9] Consequently, the judiciary in Florida appears to have been granted not only the sole adjudicatory authority, but also the responsibility for managing itself through its administrative authority.[10] A literal reading of Article V thus depicts a judicial system that rivals any in the nation for its adherence to the classical tenets of court reform.

The reform movement in Florida was later supplemented by the approval of a 1976 constitutional amendment that instituted merit selection and retention of appellate court judges. This mechanism replaces the old nonpartisan election technique and is operationalized through nominating commissions and unop-

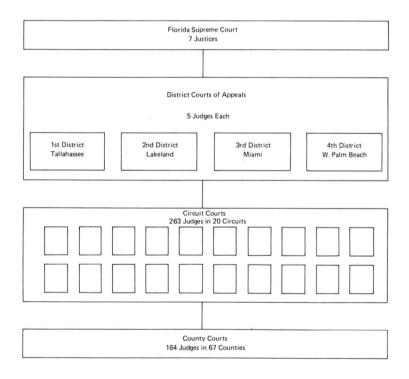

Figure 2-1. State of Florida Court Organization.

posed elections, much like the fabled "Missouri Plan."[11] Despite the apparent comprehensiveness of these alterations, court reformers soon realized that efficient administration of a court system could not be achieved by structural improvements alone. The impact of traditional modes of operation lingered and tended to inhibit the adoption of a viable system of court administration to accommodate the new structure. Thus, determination of the success of the reforms stipulated in Article V is dependent upon a consideration of the court personnel and organizations vested with responsibility for adapting the traditional managerial practices to the renovated structure.

The Chief Judges

The circuit courts are Florida's trial courts of general jurisdiction and have exclusive original jurisdiction in all actions of law not cognizable by county courts. The state is divided into twenty judicial circuits following county lines. Five of Florida's sixty-seven counties encompass an entire judicial circuit, while the remaining fifteen circuits encompass between two and seven counties (figure 2-2). The number of circuit judges authorized for each circuit varies from two to over seventy.

Circuit court judges are elected circuit-wide for six-year terms in nonpartisan elections. Vacancies are filled by the governor from recommendations submitted by nonpartisan Judicial Nominating Commissions found in each circuit. The requirements for holding office are quite modest. A judge must devote his energies solely to judicial duties and is eligible for office if he resides in the territorial jurisdiction of his circuit. The prospective judge must be an elector of the state and must have been a member of the bar of Florida for a minimum of five years. No judge can serve after reaching the age of seventy years except to complete a term of office.[12]

The chief judge of each circuit is chosen from among the judges in his jurisdiction for a term of two years. Under the Florida Rules of Procedure established by the supreme court, and as cited in Article V, the chief judge of each circuit is established as the chief administrative official for all courts within his jurisdiction. Thus, he is responsible for the supervision of all judicial and quasi-judicial activities that occur in any of the courts within his circuit.

The unitary court system instituted by Article V is hierarchically structured to give the chief justice of the supreme court final administrative authority over the actions of his subordinates. Thus, the chief judges of the twenty circuits have the responsibility to recommend to the chief justice any substantive proposal designed to expedite court administration. Any procedural, organizational, budgetary, or personnel requirements that affect the judicial system as a whole are submitted to the chief justice for review. The chief justice must then evaluate the competing requests in terms of the judicial budget in order to assure the most equitable distribution of scarce resources.

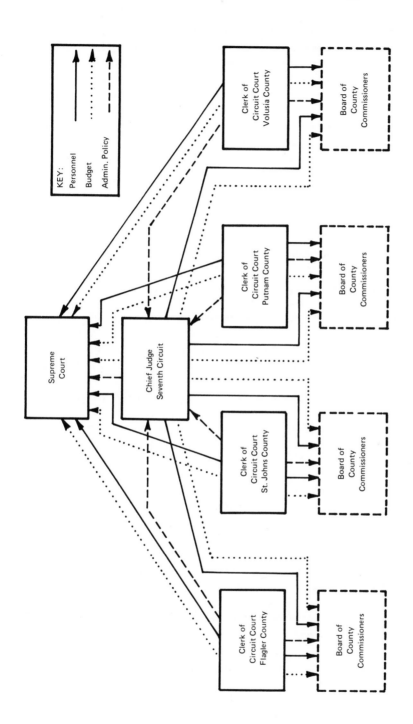

Figure 2-2. Administrative Process of a Typical Judicial Circuit.

However, most judicial management considerations that confront the chief judges are not of a nature that requires action by the chief justice. Internal budget preparation, resource allocation, rotation of judges, calendaring, assignment of space, personnel management and administration, and judicial coordination are all functions that are the direct responsibility of the chief judges. All court personnel within the circuits are administratively subservient to their respective chief judges in these matters. Consequently, the chief judge has constitutionally derived total administrative authority over most aspects of court management in his circuit. Any management question arising from a county court, clerk's office, or any other judicial or quasi-judicial agency is directly within the purview of the chief judge. Thus, these persons have the authority to undertake practically any action they deem necessary to expedite judicial business.

Consequently, the circuit court chief judges constitute key variables in examining the present judicial system in Florida. The primary responsibility for implementing Article V has been deposited squarely in their hands. Any administrative uniformity that results from the reorganization of the state's judicial system will be derived largely from their efforts. Their attempts to surmount the obstacles spawned by generations of decentralization and traditionalism will dictate the level of success that the reform movement achieves.[13] Conversely, the disinclination of the chief judges to utilize their strategic administrative positions to unify and coordinate the judicial system would indicate either that the style of reforms that were instituted do not suit Florida's situation or that the chief judges simply do not *desire* to alter the traditional methods of operation.

The chief judges were interviewed in this study in order to examine the roles and functions they have assumed in the revamped judicial structure.[14] As a group, the judges constitute a relatively homogeneous body. The typical chief judge is a Caucasian, Protestant male who has been a permanent resident of Florida. Of the sixteen judges interviewed, only one had not graduated from a law school within the state. Not surprisingly, a tremendous coincidence of political and administrative backgrounds is evident. Only two judges (12.5 percent) indicated that they had received any type of formalized administrative training. All the judges had been employed in private legal practice at one time or another before ascending the bench. The entire sample listed their political party preference as Democratic (table 2-1).

The uniformity in the background variables of the judges implies that a corresponding continuity in attitudes toward judicial roles and functions might exist. The chief judges had apparently undergone very similar socialization processes. They attended the same academic institutions, obtained nearly identical pre-entry experience, and were raised in very analogous social environments, and each had been on the bench for many years preceding the implementation of Article V. Consequently, all of the chief judges were well acquainted with the traditional modes of operation that had dominated Florida's

Table 2-1
Background Variables: Chief Judges

Variables	Number	Percentage
Age:		
31-40 years	2	12.50
41-50 years	6	37.50
51-60 years	7	43.75
Over 60 years	1	6.25
Sex:		
Female	0	0.00
Male	16	100.00
Race:		
Caucasian	16	100.00
Other	0	0.00
Religion:		
Catholic	3	18.75
Jewish	2	12.50
Protestant	11	68.75
Length of Florida Residence:		
11-20 years	1	6.25
Over 20 years	15	93.75
Administrative Experience:		
Yes	4	25.00
No	12	75.00
Political Party Preference:		
Republican	0	0.00
Democrat	16	100.00
Independent	0	0.00
Length of Tenure in Office:		
6-10 years	5	31.25
11-15 years	7	43.75
16-20 years	2	12.50
Over 20 years	2	12.50
Ideology:		
Conservative	8	50.00
Liberal	5	31.25
Moderate	3	18.75

judicial system before reorganization. Any resulting carryover of anachronistic management practices are especially germaine to this analysis.

The most obvious initial conclusion ascertained concerning the roles of the chief judges in the judicial system is that they have, for a variety of reasons, defaulted in their administrative responsibilities. Instead of assuming the burden for the managerial direction of their circuits, most chief judges seem to have perpetuated the previous system that diffused management authority. Their interview responses indicate that they tend to view their role as that of arbiters of disputes that arise within the judicial system. Although this sentiment was variously worded by the judges, the attitude appears to be relatively widespread, and few judges indicated they have actively become involved in the actual implementation of reform-oriented policies. As one judge stated, "My business is the law. My business is not to concern myself with the budgeting, calendaring, or personnel. I make the rules and orders of law." As a result of this orientation, responsibility for the daily administrative operation of the court system has been at least partially abdicated.

The authors of Article V had assumed that vesting centralized responsibility in the chief judges would enhance intercircuit coordination. However, the interviews indicate that the majority of chief judges have not assumed the duties that are prerequisites to the attainment of such a goal. According to the reform literature, coordination depends upon the development of consistent budgetary, personnel, and general management systems under the rubric of centralized authority. However, most management functions, including budgeting, space and equipment supervision, and personnel, appear to have remained in the hands of the persons who have traditionally performed such tasks. Although the chief judges exercise titular control over these activities, little active participation or policy making is evident.

This phenomenon may be partially attributed to the lingering influences of the management practices that existed before reorganization. Judges have historically been obligated to perform the role of a politician as well as that of an officer of the court, and many chief judges may still approach their jobs from a political posture. The utilization of bureaucratic practices to attain organizational goals appears to be antithetical to the judges' standards of "fair play." Thus, the use of constitutionally derived administrative powers to accomplish objectives is not considered by the judges to be an especially viable method of confronting problems. Instead, the findings of this study indicate judges tend to deal with administrative maladies on a personalistic level. Examples of such behavior are numerous. Most of the judges stated that before they make a decision influencing the activities of other administrative personnel in the system, they first consult all the interested parties and determine which course of action is most acceptable. In evaluating the characteristics most beneficial to a good judge, they placed a much greater emphasis on interpersonal skills than on managerial or administrative capabilities. Furthermore, seven judges (43.8 percent) implied that the title "chief administrator," as it relates to the chief judge, is simply a pseudonym for their role as chief political officer of the court.

Despite the pervasive degree of uniformity present among the backgrounds and attitudes of the chief judges, several notable exceptions are apparent. Some judges in large metropolitan circuits appear to be far more reform oriented than their colleagues in more rural areas. In the two largest circuits the chief judges reported they have discontinued personally hearing cases in order to devote full attention to administrative matters and that they have instituted innovative managerial procedures. For example, the judge of the largest circuit has coordinated the budgetary process between the courts and quasi-judicial agencies to such an extent that few personnel or capital expenditures may be made without his personal approval. The chief judge of another highly urbanized circuit has adopted what is termed a "managerial system." The elements of this system include: "a centralized equipment and supplies dispersal office, co-ordinated personnel and budgeting functions, and uniform management direction aimed at isolating and confronting problem areas."

As opposed to the chief judges of the larger circuits, several of the judges from rural areas appear to adhere more closely to the traditional management practices. These persons were particularly verbose concerning the impracticality of "managing" the courts. Because most of the personnel in the hierarchy are independently elected officials, several of the rural judges questioned the wisdom and legitimacy of "ordering them around." Consequently, the generally accepted management technique in these judges' circuits seems to be that of "crisis management"—when a problem arises, the chief judge will exercise his authority to alleviate the situation—and few judges indicated an interest in actively pursuing reform.

The chief judges who displayed the greatest degree of skepticism regarding Article V were primarily from rural circuits. Typical comments usually included such phrasing as the following: "Article V is an administrative boondoggle!" The chief judges who voiced sentiments of this type often implied that the imposition of an administrative system into the judicial organization "makes most judges think that someone doesn't think they're doing a good job or what's right." Moreover, these judges clearly opposed both the concept and the application of the case disposition reporting system (CDR).[15] They indicated they felt that the CDR system is inaccurate and that it represents an organizational control that does not conform to the nature of judicial tasks. By measuring the number of cases disposed by each judge and court annually, the judges believed, the CDR ignores the concept of "quality" as it relates to litigation.

Despite the negative attitudes toward Article V evident among several of the rural judges, a majority of the chief judges in the state appear to view the measure quite favorably. Most of the judges reported they were pleased with the effects of unification. By eradicating the utter fragmentation that existed before reorganization, Article V, in their view, had instituted a "streamlined" court system. Among the benefits mentioned by various chief judges were: "It makes it easier for attorneys to work across government boundaries"; "It will enable us to create more uniformity in budgeting priorities"; and "Less friction now exists because the varying jurisdictions have been consolidated." However, most of the judges acknowledged that they had not accomplished many of the goals that are within their power to pursue. The reasons cited by most judges to explain this failure of not fully exercising their administrative authority primarily revolved around political issues.

The establishment of a unified court system (which includes centralized control of personnel, budgeting, space and equipment) depends upon the acquiescence of a large number of local officials who have traditionally performed critical roles in judicial activities. Although the chief judges certainly possess the requisite power to impose their wills on these persons, the findings of this study indicate the anticipated political ramifications of such actions have inhibited them from invoking their authority. Consequently, determining the success of the reforms stipulated in Article V also requires examining the political personages whose roles overlap that of the chief judges and therefore restrict the latitude of judicial administrative behavior.

The Court Clerks

In many states clerks of the circuit courts serve as the ministerial officers for the circuit courts located within their counties. Like the court clerks in Florida prior to Article V, these persons also serve in the capacities of county recorder, county finance officer, county treasurer, county auditor, county comptroller, and secretary/accountant for the county commission. Under typical decentralized court systems, clerks are independent functionaries who are beyond most administrative supervision. The only guidance they receive is from legislative provisions and dictates from county commissions.

The clerk's office in most states constitutes the primary administrative arm of circuit courts, and as constitutionally elected officials, court clerks have traditionally exercised a great deal of discretion in the organization and operation of their offices. Freedom from judicial and executive control has enabled them to utilize whatever business methods they deem appropriate. The situation has been described thusly: "The clerks use the business procedures they find when they take office or with which they are generally familiar from other sources."[16] These practices result in a lack of uniformity, the continued use of outdated management techniques, poor organization of functions, and several other serious administrative dilemmas.

Judges have been compelled to countenance such incompetencies because the clerks represent a formidable local political power by virtue of their large number of executive and administrative duties. Since the courts depend upon the county for appropriations to finance judicial activities, judges, including those in Florida, for obvious reasons have been hesitant to demand more professional behavior from the clerks. Consequently, most judges have responded to this situation by developing political competence in their dealings with these local officials.

The constitutional role of the Florida clerks in the judicial process has been greatly *expanded* by Article V. Instead of simply retaining responsibility for the administrative functions of the circuit courts, under Article V the clerks have also been assigned responsibility for performing all the clerical functions of the courts that have been consolidated into the two-tier structure. Moreover, while their judicial role has been increased tremendously, with few exceptions the clerks have not been divested of their county-based functions.[17]

The court clerks in Florida campaign on a county-wide partisan ballot for four-year terms. The only requirements for holding office are that the person must be an elector of the state and must devote his full attention to the duties of the post. Court clerks' salaries range from approximately $15,000 to $32,000, depending upon the population of their respective counties.

The present organization of the clerks' offices generally follows the pattern that existed prior to the revision of Article V. In sixty-four counties the court functions are currently grouped with the county fiscal and recording functions. Although Section 16 of Article V made severing the nonjudicial functions from the clerks' offices possible, only three counties have done so.[18] Consequently, two distinct organizational models of the clerks' offices exist (figures 2-3 and 2-4). The failure to separate the two sets of duties and responsibilities has enabled a large majority of the clerks to retain a prominent role in the administrative operation of the judicial system and has thus resulted in an oxymoronic situation. While the chief judges have been granted titular administrative authority over the entire circuit judicial system, the structural alterations required to consolidate this power have not been instituted. The court clerks continue to occupy positions from which they can potentially challenge the authority of the chief judges. The extent to which the clerks exercise this prerogative, and thus inhibit the coordinating functions of the chief judges, must be analyzed in terms of such variables as their perceived roles and duties as judicial actors.

The court clerks interviewed in this study constitute a group that is almost as homogeneous as that of the chief judges (table 2-2).[19] In fact, an enormous degree of uniformity is present in the socio-economic characteristics of the clerks. In the entire sample of fifty-seven respondents there is not a single non-Caucasian. The majority of the clerks are over the age of fifty, have agrarian backgrounds, and now occupy the only public office they have ever sought. Fifty-five (96.5 percent) of the clerks are males, and fifty-two (91.2 percent) are Protestants. Most clerks have been life-long residents of the state.

Florida has traditionally been a "one-party state." As in most Southern states, the Democratic party has dominated since Reconstruction. The interview responses of the clerks indicate that this domination by the Democrats is not in serious jeopardy. Almost 90 percent of the respondents are Democrats, and as might be expected from the background data, forty-eight (84.2 percent) stated that they adhere to a conservative political philosophy. Consequently, as has been stated in an essay by William C. Havard, "the social and/or economic

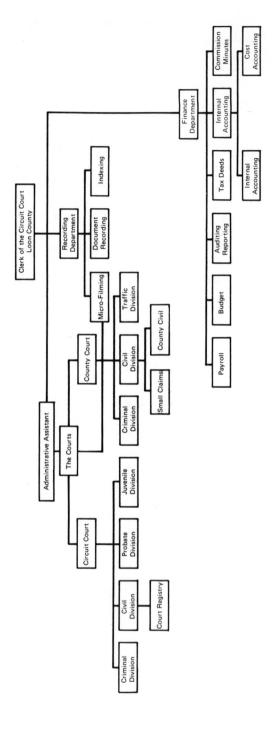

Figure 2-3. Traditional Organizational Model: Clerk of the Circuit Court.

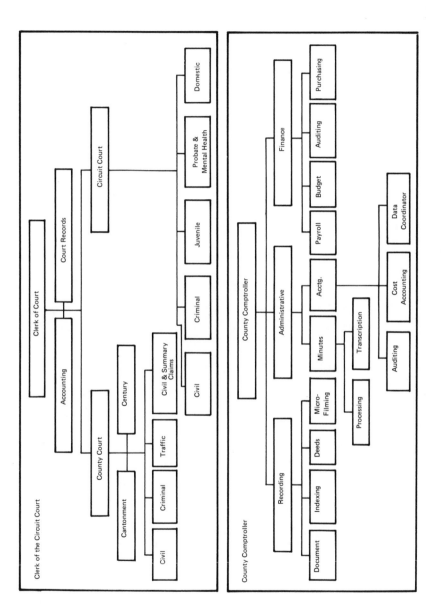

Figure 2-4. Reformed Organizational Model: Two Officers.

Table 2-2
Background Variables: Court Clerks

Variables	Number	Percentage
Age:		
Less than 31 years	1	1.8
31-40 years	8	14.0
41-50 years	13	22.8
51-60 years	24	42.1
Over 60 years	11	19.3
Sex:		
Female	2	3.5
Male	55	96.5
Race:		
Caucasian	57	100.0
Other	0	0.0
Religion:		
Catholic	3	5.3
Jewish	0	0.0
Protestant	52	91.2
Other	2	3.5
Length of Florida Residence:		
6-10 years	1	1.8
11-20 years	2	3.5
Over 20 years	54	94.7
Extent of Education:		
Some high school	1	1.8
High school diploma	20	35.0
2 years of college	15	26.3
4 year college degree	9	15.8
Some graduate work	7	12.3
Master's degree	5	8.8
Length of Tenure in Office:		
1-5 years	15	26.3
6-10 years	9	15.8
Over 10 years	33	57.9
Political Party Preference:		
Republican	8	14.0
Democrat	48	84.2
Independent	1	1.8
Ideology:		
Conservative	50	87.7
Liberal	4	7.0
Moderate	2	3.5
Unrecorded	1	1.8

'liberal' is a rarity among contemporary Florida office-holders."[20] The consequences of this apparent uniformity in political and ideological characteristics were aptly reviewed in Havard's essay: "Florida's political relations are highly personalized. Office politics predominate over issues, with the result that policy is worked out interpersonally among the office-holders after the election."[21] Havard concludes that this phenomenon results in decidedly local orientations in Florida's political ethos and a corresponding inconsistency in political groupings.[22]

The predominance of personalistic and/or political interrelationships that are characteristic of the chief judges reappears in the activities of the clerks. These factors indicate that the majority of court clerks have a decidedly localistic orientation. When asked to specify their most important duty, 47 percent of the clerks specifically stated that such functions as "serving the local electorate" and "assisting the county commission" take precedence over any other. Many other clerks expressed concern over Article V because they fear that centralization will deny local citizens a "responsive" judiciary. Expecting the clerks to display any other types of attitudes may be unreasonable, for although court clerks are constitutionally required to respond to both the county and the court as distinct policy-making entities, "their predominant identification as county officers is virtually guaranteed because the county provides most of their operating revenues."[23] Moreover, the clerks are elected by county and consequently depend upon a satisfied electorate to insure their continued tenure.

The localistic orientation of the court clerks affects their actual and perceived roles and duties within the court system in a number of ways. For example, 65 percent of the clerks noted that they neither presently use, nor intend to use, any type of technological innovation to expedite their court-related duties. The rationale of most of these clerks was that such management aids are expensive and are therefore not in the best interests of their constituents. In addition, some chief judges complained that clerks often coalesce with the county commissions to defeat increased budgetary appropriations for the court system. The extent to which administrative efficiency is relegated to a role secondary to that of political expediency thus becomes a function of the clerks' conceptions of their roles as judicial officers.

The personal values any person holds will obviously influence the occupational role orientation and the policies advocated by that person.[24] As both a county and judicial officer, the typical clerk is subject to a great deal of role conflict between these two competing occupational positions. According to Thomas Henderson, "The heads of all bureaucratic agencies must resolve conflicts between their roles as bureaucratic administrators and as major policy advisors."[25] As many authors have noted, occupants of such offices resolve this conflict by either becoming more involved in local politics or by viewing themselves as professionals and thereby devoting themselves to objective standards of performance at the expense of local support.[26] As has been stated, most clerks in this study seem to identify with local power structures. Their concern with limiting expenditures and pleasing their electorates and county commissions is documented.

However, the survey data reveals that most clerks also perceived themselves to be crucial administrative officers of the court. Among their responses that reflect this attitude are the following: "I'm the main wheel"; "I'm the hub around which the entire court structure revolves"; and "The clerks' offices are the information and mechanical center of the judicial system." Sixty-three percent of the clerks specifically envisioned their role in the court system as being "vital" or "crucial." The remaining clerks indicated that their roles involve major substantive areas of administration such as budgeting and personnel management for the courts.

Thus, the clerks appear to be especially plagued by role conflict: On the one hand, they generally ascribe to a parochial orientation; yet on the other hand, they consider themselves to be critical administrative officers of the court. Since the judges, by their own admission, have failed to exercise requisite control over the activities of clerks, the affect this dichotomous role perception has on the administrative efficiency sought under Article V depends ultimately upon the degree of professionalism present among the clerks. To the extent that the clerks display the characteristics of professionalism, the impact of the localistic orientation can be expected to be buffered. Thus, professional standards of objectivity represent the only effective control on the behavior of clerks as it relates to court administration.

The variables used in this study as indicators of the emphasis given to professionalism by the clerks include: educational achievement, extent of training and experience in administration, attendance at training programs, and recruitment and training requirements of court employees. At first glance these indicators show that the clerks are a relatively professional group. The study revealed that the clerks as a whole are moderately well educated. Sixty-one percent reported they have at least a high school education or some college training (see table 2-2), and 37 percent have obtained college degrees or have completed some postgraduate work. Additionally, 35 percent of the clerks indicated that they have received some type of administrative experience or training. Finally, fifty-one clerks (89.5 percent) have attended court management training seminars that are conducted periodically by the State Clerks' Association.

However, closer scrutiny of the responses indicates that the initial impressions of the clerks' degree of professionalism are not particularly justified. A majority of the administrative training and experience received by the clerks has not been court oriented. Only five clerks responded that they had received any court-related training or experience prior to assuming office, while the remainder of the clerks realized their pre-entry administrative training primarily in private business enterprises. Although almost all court clerks reported attending the court management seminars, the nature of instruction received at these gatherings is rarely pertinent to court administration. Rather, the seminars often constitute social and political convocations where the clerks discuss mutual problems and political strategies. The number of clerks who have attended Institute for Court Management programs is especially significant. The institute is the major professionally oriented training program for court managers presently in existence. Only three court clerks (5.3 percent) reported attending any of the clinics offered by the institute.

Perhaps the most revealing indicator of the clerks' professional orientations appears in the personnel practices employed in their organizations. The vast majority of clerks' offices reported they do not require the deputy clerks to undergo any type of formalized training. In fact, only a few clerks indicated they have instituted instructional programs for recently employed deputies. Obviously, employees of most clerks must thus rely upon being "broken in" by the personnel they are replacing.

Analysis of the indicators thus reveals that the court clerks, as a group, do not merit classification as "professionals." Without the restraint of professional standards, or close supervision by the chief judges, clerks are ostensibly free of organizational controls. This fact is exceedingly noteworthy because the clerks' offices employ by far the largest number of judicial personnel and expend 70 percent of the entire court system budget annually. They thus occupy a position from which their inaction, or their actions working in contradistinction to those of the chief judges, can subvert the operation of the entire judicial system.

The perceived importance of this position to the clerks was evidenced by their defensiveness. During the course of this study, efforts were made to interview a number of deputy clerks throughout Florida. However, of the thirty clerks' offices initially contacted or visited, only five permitted their assistants either to be interviewed or to complete questionnaires. The explanations offered by the clerks for their refusals typically included the statement, "They can't tell you anything that I can't." A large number of clerks also indicated they were very concerned that their own responses to the questionnaires would remain innominate. Although a multitude of explanations could be offered for this defensive attitude, the most pertinent rationale appears to be linked to the creation of the Office of State Courts Administrator. Recurring complaints by the court clerks indicated that they felt the supreme court, through the administrator's office, was attempting to wrest the clerks' control of the administrative functions from them. As one clerk stated, "Anyone coming around here lately makes us edgy." Thus the clerks apparently feared anyone who might have been collecting information that could be used as "ammunition" against them.

Although a majority of the clerks appear to be rather parochial, unprofessional, and defensive, this phenomenon is by no means universal. As with the judges, the clerks from urban areas are generally more professional than their rural colleagues. The more highly educated clerks also appear to be much more progressive than the norm. An interesting finding is that the clerks in these two groupings have developed management styles very different from many other clerks. There is a high correlation between education and delegation of judicial authority. The more highly educated clerks, on the whole, have internally divested themselves of court functions and have appointed "judicial assistants" to assume those duties. However, this group of clerks is clearly in the minority. The findings of this study indicate that most court clerks continue to exercise a degree of influence and control over court administration that rivals that of their predecessors of past decades.

Court Executive Assistants

Developments in court administration have progressed at a rapid rate during the past twenty-five years. One of the most innovative approaches to the solution of judicial problems has been the creation of a professional group of trained court executives to assist judges in their administrative duties. Reformers assume that persons who are competent both in management procedures and in judicial process will bring needed expertise and innovation to the courts. Although the persons who occupy these positions have been referred to by a number of titles, the most common are "court administrator," "court executive," "judicial administrator," or "court executive assistant."

Since 1950, the growth of the court administrator profession has been dramatic. Nearly every state presently employs a state court administrator to assist the chief justice and the state supreme court in their administrative functions. Moreover, trial court administrators are utilized in almost all metropolitan jurisdictions.[27] Despite the rapid increase in their numbers, many court administrators have experienced difficulty in gaining significant administrative responsibility. In addition, many trial court judges refuse to hire court administrators, especially in the rural areas. A partial explanation for the hesitancy of many trial level judges to fully utilize the services of court administrators is that the duties assigned to such personnel have traditionally been the province of court clerks. Consequently, the services offered by the administrators are often regarded by judges as being unnecessary.

A large number of authorities in the literature on court management discuss in great detail what the hypothesized functions and roles of trial level court executives should be.[28] The most widely accepted delineation of these duties and responsibilities expected of such personnel appears in the *Standards Relating to Court Organization*. The *Standards* state that court administrators should be responsible for: calendar management, administration of staff services, personnel and financial management, records management, liaison with the public and other government agencies, and secretariat functions for judges' meetings and the like.[29] The *Standards* also designate that an "Executive Director," or a state-wide court administrator, should be appointed by the highest appeals court of every state to create and implement uniform administrative procedures.[30] According to the *Standards*, each local administrator is to be responsible for supervising the implementation of the standardized personnel, budgeting, information, and records-management systems designed by the centralized director. The individual trial level court executives are to be supervised by the state level administrator who is responsible only to the state's highest court. Consequently, presently accepted definitions of the court administrator's duties are devised to centralize, coordinate, and standardize the entire administrative operation of the judicial system. Thus, the acceptance of a viable professional corps of judicial executives by a state is predicated on the elimination of the administration functions from traditional court managers. Since the executives' duties include the supervision of the entire support staff of each court, there can be no allowance for the existence of competing management authority other than the concurrent responsibility of chief judges.

Although the number of court administrators employed throughout the nation has been increasing dramatically, the general concept has not enjoyed an abundance of success. Administrators in many courts are not accorded the duties and responsibilities that are required to achieve their intended goal. Many judges have been reluctant to delegate authority to these personnel. As one judge has reportedly stated, "The idea of a court administrator was conjured up as an assault on judicial independence and an attempt to demean the status of the judge to that of a glorified civil servant."[31] Consequently, many professional managers have been given control over little more than statistics-gathering functions. The vested interests of court clerks and other personnel who have historically been involved in court management have also served to inhibit and delay the acceptance of the profession.

In Florida, there is a state-wide court administrator directly under the supervision of the chief justice of the supreme court. The Office of State Courts Administrator was created by supreme court rule in July 1972 to "assist the Chief Justice in his capacity as the chief administrative office of the state judicial system."[32] Since that time, seventeen trial court administrators have been employed by the circuit courts. The organization of the administrative system established among these administrators closely parallels that outlined in the ABA *Standards*. The central administrator's office is charged with the responsibility of creating uniform standards of administration to be applied throughout the state; the circuit administrators are theoretically responsible for implementing and supervising these management procedures within their respective circuits.

Court executives are appointed by the chief judges. The state-wide administrator is appointed by the chief justice of the Florida Supreme Court, with the concurrence of the other members of that body. The state administrative office is located in the supreme court building and employs a staff of approximately thirty persons, both professional and clerical. Conversely, many circuit administrators are limited to only one assistant, their secretary. However, a few of the court executives situated in larger circuits have as many as twenty or more administrative assistants.

The data gathered in this study show that most professional court administrators in Florida are eminently qualified to manage judicial systems. Ten administrators (71.4 percent) hold college degrees. Eight (57.2 percent) have either obtained graduate degrees or are curently working toward an advanced diploma (table 2-3). Of the fourteen executives who responded to the questionnaire, ten (71.4 percent) were employed in court-related administrative positions before being appointed to their present offices. Most of these administrators had been prosecutors, juvenile court administrators, deputy clerks of circuit courts, or law enforcement supervisors. Moreover, twelve (85.8 percent) have undergone some type of court-related administrative training since assuming their present positions. Nine (64.3 percent) have attended one or more of the training sessions offered by the Institute of Court Management.

The court executives are a rather homogeneous group. All are Caucasian males who have resided in Florida for most of their adult lives. Most are Protestants who have few ethnic ties and whose backgrounds are primarily middle class. Only five administrators (35.7 percent) adhere to a conservative social and political philosophy, although only one stated that he is a Republican. With one exception, all administrators receive an annual salary of over $20,000.

Background characteristics of the court executives interviewed in this study indicate that they are less parochial and less conservative than their colleagues, the court clerks. As a group they are better educated and have received a greater level of court-related experience and training. Partially due to their pre-entry experiences, the administrators might be expected to have developed comparatively greater professional orientations toward their responsibilities, and since they are appointed officials, their allegiance to the judicial system should be assured. The court administrators are not required to please an interested electorate in order to retain their positions as are the clerks. Consequently, these personnel should represent a major cosmopolitan force in the judicial structure and as such might be expected to be a crucial variable in attempts to overcome the traditional fragmentation that has restrained reform movements in the past.

However, early in the investigation the fact became apparent that court administrators in Florida presently do not represent a viable instrument of court reform in many cases. They have been generally unsuccessful in consolidating their positions and in initiating the uniform administrative standards advocated by the Office of State Courts Administrator. The explanation for this failure on the part of the circuit court administrators to achieve the intended goals of the authors of Article V is linked to their perceived roles and duties, as well as to the reception given them by the traditional court managers.

When asked to specify their most important duty, only two administrators (14.3 percent) mentioned functional aspects of court administration such as budget preparation or case flow management. Conversely, five administrators stated that "assisting the judge" is their most significant function. The remaining

Table 2-3
Background Variables: Court Administrators

Variables	Number	Percentage
Age:		
31-40 years	2	14.3
41-50 years	6	42.9
51-60 years	5	35.7
Over 60 years	1	7.1
Sex:		
Female	0	0.0
Male	14	100.0
Race:		
Caucasian	14	100.0
Other	0	0.0
Religion:		
Catholic	1	7.1
Jewish	1	7.1
Protestant	10	71.4
Unrecorded	2	14.3
Length of Florida Residence:		
1-5 years	2	14.3
6-10 years	2	14.3
11-20 years	1	7.1
Over 20 years	9	64.3
Extent of Education:		
Some high school	1	7.1
High school diploma	1	7.1
2 years of college	2	14.3
4 year college degree	2	14.3
Some graduate work	4	28.6
Master's degree	2	14.3
Law degree	2	14.3
Attendance at ICM Seminars:		
Yes	10	71.4
No	4	28.6
Political Party Preference:		
Republican	1	7.1
Democrat	9	64.3
Independent	2	14.3
Unrecorded	2	14.3
Ideology:		
Conservative	5	35.7
Liberal	4	28.6
Moderate	2	14.3
Unrecorded	3	21.4

administrators listed abstract concepts such as "communication" and "co-ordination." The court executives' perceptions of their roles are even more revealing. Nine administrators (69.3 percent) viewed themselves as "the judge's right hand man." Assisting the chief judge in coordinating the elements of the judicial system thus appears to be the primary role perception of these personnel. Accordingly, most court administrators noted that their role in the judicial system is quite passive. As one administrator stated: "The judges assign us very few tasks. Don't rock the boat, so to speak, is the most fundamental rule."

The problems that the court administrators regarded as most serious are useful in explicating their passive role orientation. When asked to delineate their primary occupational dilemmas, the following responses were given most often: "Procuring the cooperation of various county commissions and other county officers"; "handling the personalities and biases of numerous judges"; "strong objections to change"; "misunderstandings between agencies as to the role, function, and effect of court administrators"; and "obtaining the acceptance of the court administrator concept by judges and clerks." These statements indicate that the court administrators felt opposed on several fronts: Apparently, many judges, clerks, and local political bodies either do not comprehend the purpose of their profession or simply objected to the court administrator concept as defined by the ABA *Standards.* Whatever the reason, the court administrators believed that they had few "friends" in the local political and judicial systems. Consequently, most appear to have opted for a passive role that would reduce the likelihood that they would further alienate any specific group. One administrator summarized his feelings thusly: "In order to make any advances in court administration we have to remain low key and simply try to obtain authority through competence."[33]

In determining the actual impact court administrators are likely to have on the judicial system, the attitudes of the court clerks and judges toward them are important. Since court administrators represent what might be termed the "embodiment of reform" and have been associated with, and a part of, every major judicial reform movement of the past decade, the attitudes of clerks and judges toward them are viewed in this study as possible indicators of the predispositions these two groups hold toward reform in general.

A utilitarian indicator of the chief judges' conception of the court administrators is the techniques they utilize in selecting persons to occupy the positions. Several judges admitted that they had hired specific administrators on the basis of personal acquaintance and friendship. For example, two adminis-trators were undergraduate classmates of the chief judges who appointed them. Another chief judge was reputed by his successor to have appointed a "crony" ex-county judge who had been defeated in the previous election. Another instance of amicism was reported in one circuit where the judges experienced a serious altercation in attempting to decide between two candidates for the position: One had been a college friend of the appointing judge; the second was the son-in-law of another judge. All but three court administrators reported that they had known their appointing chief judge personally before their appointments.

The rationales offered by the chief judges to explain this phenomenon would seem to be based on their perceptions of the qualities a court administrator should possess. The judges repeatedly stated that in their opinions a court administrator must be a person who has great interpersonal skills and who is familiar with the personnel within the judicial system. Moreover, a "general working knowledge" of judicial systems was also regarded as an important prerequisite to employment. These attitudes indicate that most chief judges selected personal acquaintances whose knowledge of the individual circuits was recognized. Although no judge would admit that the selection of such a person was a convenient method of assuring control, the implication is obvious.

A second useful indicator of the chief judges' attitudes toward the court administrators and toward their own roles in the reform process is provided by examining the specific duties and responsibilities they have delegated to their administrators. The trend among most chief judges is to delegate whatever administrative minutia the judge does not have time to do. Consequently, court administrators commonly prepare the calendar, manage courtroom space and equipment, supervise the court personnel within the immediate office, and make recommendations to the chief judges. Every chief judge reported giving his administrator total responsibility for the case disposition reporting system, but few report asking their administrators to assume authority over clerical personnel, records management, or the total circuit budget, the traditional domain of court clerks.

An interesting finding of the research is that a few chief judges appear to view their court administrators as personal valets provided at state expense. In fact, one instance was discovered in which a convalescing judge utilized the services of his court executive to chauffer him to judicial conferences and other judicial functions. One judge, while extolling the virtues of the court administrator concept, explained how his own administrator was quite useful in "arranging the investitures, getting the robes, and fixing up the offices" of newly elected judges.

At the time the research was conducted, three judges did not utilize court administrators; they all stated that because the crucial court personnel are elected, they could not "expect an appointed administrator to tell a sheriff, clerk or judge what to do." With no legitimate authority over such personnel, the administrator is viewed by these judges as performing the functions of a "glorified secretary." Moreover, two of these judges had misgivings about the state courts administrator. These judges clearly feared that particular central administrator was developing a strong power base in Tallahassee from which he would "take over if the wrong man is made Chief Justice," and they reported resisting the placement of court executives in their circuits for this reason even though the "pressure" from Tallahassee was occasionally severe.

Although most chief judges have failed to utilize their administrators effectively, the liability for this phenomenon cannot be entirely assigned to the judges. As one chief judge stated, "When I tried to separate the clerks' offices in this circuit and give the judicial functions to the administrator, the clerks screamed." This comment reflects a reality that all the chief judges have been compelled to confront. Some clerks clearly regarded the creation of the court administrator's position in the circuits as a threat to their role in the administrative process.

The extent to which some court clerks interviewed in this study object to court administrators is readily apparent. Forty-nine percent (28) of the clerks indicated they did not believe that court administrators perform a useful function. Adjectives such as "useless," "worthless," and "incompetent" were often used to describe the court executives. Among some of the comments are the following: "He simply collects his checks"; "I haven't been able to find out anything he does"; "He doesn't know nothing [sic] about the courts"; "I know of little that he does that we [the clerks] do not or cannot do, and at less expense to the taxpayer"; "The clerks and sheriffs can do this [the administrator's duties], especially in small or medium size counties"; and "he does nothing a good secretary can't do."

Despite these negative sentiments, twenty-nine (50.0 percent adjusted frequency) of the clerks did state that the administrator performs some type of useful function. Sixteen of this group remarked that the data collection activities of the court administrators were what they perceived as being the most beneficial useful function. Other comments indicate that many clerks were perfectly content with the status quo—that is, with the court administrators as currently utilized. For example, eight respondents mentioned the court executives' duties as a "go between" and "assistant" to the chief judge as being worthwhile.

When the court clerks were asked to state whether the court administrators' offices should be strengthened, weakened, abolished, or left untouched, the responses paralleled their perceptions of the administrators' functions. Fourteen (25 percent) felt that the office should be left intact. Twenty-nine (51.8 percent) indicated they would like to see the position abolished, while only two (3.6 percent) desired to have the office weakened. Finally, eleven (19.6 percent) felt that the administrator should be given more authority and responsibility.

The clerks' attitudes toward the court administrators appears to have affected the working relationships between the two groups. The findings of this study show that many clerks circumvent the court administrator and take problems or information they have directly to the chief judges. Fifty-three percent ($N = 30$) of the clerks indicated that they do not provide the administrator with information relevant to the efficient operation of the court.

Seventy-six percent ($N = 43$) of the clerks stated that they regularly deliver such communications to the chief judge, and 80 percent ($N = 46$) reported that they conduct business with the administrator fewer than five times a month.

Nevertheless, very little overt friction appears to occur between the clerks and administrators. Only six clerks (12 percent adjusted frequency) indicated that there is any real friction between their offices and those of the administrators. A typical response to questions concerning this issue is: "Why should there be any friction; I never see him." The clerks who did signify that friction exists made comments that indicate personality and/or personal conflicts exist between themselves and the administrators. The clerks were asked to rate the administrators according to such judgmental criteria as "bad or good," "weak or strong," and "competent or incompetent." The six clerks whose responses deviated most from the normally positive replies of their colleagues are the same clerks who reported friction in their relationships with the administrators. Although one can only conjecture as to the cause of this friction, the responses of the administrators involved to the same questions provide some insight. As one administrator said, "There is a great deal of friction between us because my secretary was an unsuccessful opponent of the clerk in the last election for the office he now holds." The five other administrators who signified that friction exists related it to such factors as "role definition," "the threat of my office," and "resentment when the judge takes my side of an issue."

In summary, the clerks' attitudes toward the administrators were found to be generally negative: Those clerks who do not openly oppose the administrator in their circuits simply disregard them. The administrators clearly represent a threat to the role perceptions and organizational positions of a number of the clerks. Consequently, the administrators, and the reforms they advocate, are likely to be resisted.

This situation is aggravated by the strategic political position of the clerks. Their access to the chief judges is assured as long as they retain control over much of the judicial support system. This system obviously compels the judges to avoid antagonizing the clerks. The extent to which the clerks value their positive relationships with chief judges is illustrated in the data: Only two clerks indicated that their affiliation with the chief judge is anything less than satisfactory. In fact, thirty-three clerks (37.9 percent) stated that their relationships with the chief judges are "excellent," and thirteen (22.8 percent) rated theirs as "very good." Moreover, there appears to exist a reciprocal attitude on the part of the judges. Only three of the judges who were interviewed made any disparaging remarks concerning the clerks personally or their performance as quasi-judicial officers. Consequently, the typical administrator must compete for duties and responsibilities with an official who is generally quite friendly with his immediate superior.

The extent to which these relationships and attitudes affect the court administrators and the reform measures they embody is significant. Because the imposition of radically innovative administrative procedures, such as centralized budgeting and personnel systems, depends upon the cooperation of all court managers, the incidence of conflict and nonsynergetic activity in the system suggests that reform will be delayed.

Administrative Process

Although Article V places ultimate administrative responsibility for the Florida court in the chief justice, authority and responsibility for quotidian management is situated at the local level.[34] In creating and designating administrative officers for the circuit court subsystems, Article V grants to chief judges, court clerks, and court administrators a great deal of discretionary power. Thus, local judicial officials play a significant role in helping to formulate state-wide administrative policies. Moreover, these personnel are given wide latitude in the execution of such policies in order to adapt them to the unique requirements of each subsystem.[35] This general arrangement is endorsed by most reform commissions and is employed in a majority of reformed state court structures.

The administrative process of the Florida judicial system must therefore be analyzed in terms of the interactions between local and state officials. The most fundamental aspect of this relationship is that most administrative policy is formulated at the local level and then is submitted to the chief justice for final review and approval.[36] However, the administrative process is much more complex than the simple hierarchical description indicates; fully grasping the intricacy of the process requires examining each of the three major components individually: the budget, personnel, and administrative processes.

The supreme court and the four district courts of appeal are all fully funded by the state government. The budgetary process of these courts is therefore very uncomplicated. The chief judges of the appellate courts submit their budgetary requests to the chief justice, who then decides final monetary priorities. However, Chapter 216 of the *Florida Statutes* requires the judiciary to submit its budget to the governor for review, modification, and incorporation into the overall state budget. The Department of Administration (the state equivalent to the federal Office of Management and Budget) has been given authority to review and alter judicial budgetary requests. The policy decisions of this agency are then submitted to the legislature for final action.[37]

The trial level courts, which are responsible for the greatest bulk of the judicial system's work load and which consume the vast majority of the judicial budget, are almost totally financed by the individual counties. The chief judges of the circuit courts submit their budgetary requests both to the court clerks and to the chief justice. Appropriations for support personnel, operating expenses, space, and equipment are generally reviewed by the court clerks and then offered to the county commissions for final approval. The chief justice considers only requests that are directly related to the circuit court offices, such as financing for additional judges and secretaries. Consequently, the circuit courts are primarily dependent upon the counties for appropriations.[38]

This reliance upon the county commissions for resources also extends into the area of personnel. However, the Department of Administration also assumes a preeminent role in this domain. The clerks of the circuit courts must obtain approval of both the county commissions and the state Department of Administration in order to employ additional personnel. Moreover, the supreme court and the other appellate courts are equally dependent upon the Department of Administration. They too must submit all personnel requests to that agency. Consequently, the judiciary of Florida is placed in the statutory role of a state agency.[39] The judicial branch must seek the approval of both the executive and legislative branches of government for financial and personnel supports. Moreover, the court clerks and county commissions must also be receptive to judicial requests in order to assure a proper level of financing. The complexity of these budgetary and personnel processes reflect the degree to which the chief justice is limited in his authority. The county commissions, legislature, and governor are all intricately involved in interpreting policy and setting priorities for the judicial branch. Therefore, fixing accountability for the operation of the court system is extremely difficult because direct lines of authority and responsibility do not exist.[40] The implications and consequences of this fragmented process are discussed in the following chapter.

The procedures utilized in implementing general administrative policies are somewhat less complicated. Most procedural and administrative rules and orders emanate from the offices of the chief judges. Therefore, each circuit chief judge has primary responsibility for determining the administrative policy that governs court reporters, judicial assignments, circuit organization, and a tremendous variety of other procedural and operational concerns. However, most chief judges in larger systems have delegated responsibility for the individual civil, criminal, probate, and other divisions to circuit judges who have been appointed "administrative judges" of those departments. Consequently, the administrative judges formulate many policies governing their individual divisions and submit them to the chief judge for approval. The court administrators are also expected to formulate potential policies and to "suggest" these to the chief judge. Through this management process the chief judges presumably hope to assure coordination and control within the circuits. Moreover, the chief justice requires that all court rules established by the circuit courts be submitted to the supreme court for review and approval. Therefore, continuity both within the circuits, and within the state judicial system as a whole, is facilitated (figure 2-5).

Summary

Despite the partial implementation of Article V, the data indicates that the Florida judicial system remains fragmented. Several competing judicial authori-

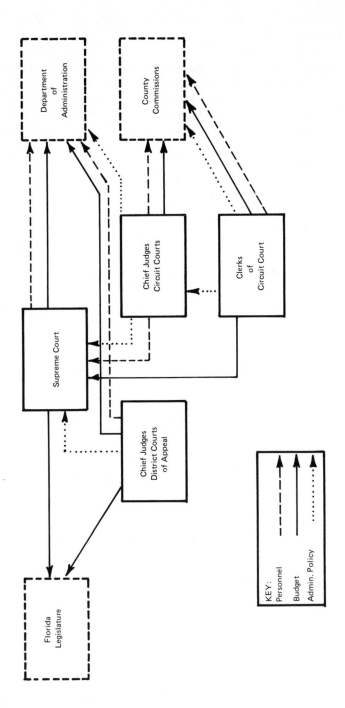

Figure 2-5. Florida State Court System Administrative Process.

ties are present. Because the chief judges have not fully operationalized the intent of Article V, the court clerks serve to diffract responsibility and authority from the court structure as a whole. The fault does not lie entirely with the chief judges, however, for many requisite aspects of viable reform have not been instituted. The judges are compelled to countenance the present organizational scheme because control over much of the judicial support system, including budgeting and personnel, has not been assumed by the state government.

Consequently, the court clerks have retained their traditional role in court administration. The inability or unwillingness of the chief judges to enforce systematic administrative standards on the clerks permits several potentially negative phenomena to exist. The court clerks are fraught by role conflict and a general lack of professional standards. Their loyalties are divided between the judicial system and the exigencies of county government. Since professionalism does not represent an effective control over their activities, the consequences for enlightened court management are severe. In addition, court administrators, who represent a potential modernizing force have not been effectively utilized. Their professional position has been subverted by a combination of resistance from court clerks and apathy from chief judges. The following chapter analyzes several of the consequences of the diffracted nature of administrative responsibility in judicial structure, as well as other implications of the incomplete state of unification in Florida.

3

The Management Dilemmas

Lack of Judicial Management

A major conclusion reached in the preceding chapter is that most chief judges have not actively attempted to consolidate the authority granted to them by Article V. Instead of firmly establishing their authority over all phases of court administration, chief judges have deferred to more parochial court managers, court clerks. Consequently, the local political environment continues to exert tremendous influence on the court system. Judicial staffs, budgets, and management policies are largely dominated by officials whose primary allegiance is to the local political community. Responsibility for court administration is thus divided between two factions that often possess conflicting orientations and goals regarding court functions.

In order to provide the consistent and uniform administrative direction that is ostensibly the intent of Article V, chief judges must be willing and able to assert their constitutional authority over the judicial bureaucracy. When court clerks and county commissioners establish court management priorities, inconsistency and inefficiency in the application of administrative practices and procedures are potentially increased. However, several aspects of the chief judges' administrative role potentially inhibit effective management and transform the position of "chief administrative officer" into a debilitated facsimile of that described in Article V.

As has been previously stated, reorganization of the Florida judicial system has not altered the intimate traditional relationship between county and court. Because counties continue to exercise tremendous discretionary power in most aspects of court administration, chief judges are compelled to rely upon political strategies and relationships in order to maintain their courts. Consequently, few judges have aggressively advocated and/or instituted comprehensive administrative programs designed to standardize and modernize management procedures within their circuits. However, the courts' reliance upon counties for financial and administrative supports is not the exclusive cause of the chief judges' reluctance to assume preeminent control over judicial machinery. Of potential importance are: (1) the elective nature of their offices; (2) their length of tenure as administrative officials; (3) the nature of their tasks; and (4) their level of managerial competence.

The first theoretical impediment to the assertive administration of state court systems arises as a result of popular election of judges. Presently, twenty-nine states elect judges on either partisan or nonpartisan ballots.[1] As Dorothy Nelson states: "The inevitable sacrifice of judicial independence is the high cost of electing judges, for judges must be responsive to the forces which place them in office and which can remove them from office."[2] According to this logic, elected judges are potentially much more susceptible to dysfunctional local influences than are their appointed colleagues. Moreover, elected judges are subject to a variety of maladies that conceivably influence their administrative capabilities. They may not adequately perform their management duties if they require the support of their colleagues for reelection. In addition, the chief judges' administrative duties may openly clash with politically "popular" activities that insure their continued tenure.[3] The fact has also been noted that elected judges under the supervision of a centralized administrative authority are often quite reluctant to submit to their superiors' control.[4] Resistance to the directives of superiors is "justified" by the argument that the judge must remain administratively independent in order to retain his judgmental independence.[5]

Interviews with chief judges in Florida indicate that the incidence of such an orientation is not unknown. For example, two chief judges commented that they occasionally have difficulty "convincing" a fellow judge to accept a transfer to another department or jurisdiction. The local judge often believes that his primary responsibility is to the circuit in which he was elected. Reticence to accept transfer to another department is occasionally attributed to the belief that the judge will be less able to meet the needs of, or be responsive to, his electorate.

Despite the fact that political considerations exert a sizable amount of influence on the activities of Florida's judges, there are few indications that blatant partisanship is present. Although all of the chief judges are Democrats, they are only tangentially related to the party organization. Incumbent circuit judges are very rarely opposed for reelection.[6] While four chief judges (25 percent) have previously held elected offices, only three (18.8 percent) have been appointed to any public position. These factors reflect a relatively low level of partisan involvement. Consequently, most of the "political" relationships of chief judges would seem to involve simple power confrontations with other elected officials rather than encompassing the sordid "party politics" normally cited as justification for appointing judges.

The second major factor that is profoundly significant in complicating the chief judges' administrative responsibilities is that the judges serve only brief two-year terms as administrative officials. Although a few chief judges are elected to more than one consecutive term, many await the termination of their period in office with undisguised relish. While an assortment of explanations may be offered for this phenomenon, the most pertinent is that administrative duties consume inordinate amounts of the chief judges' time, and in larger circuits little or no opportunity remains for judicial decision making. One judge stated, for example: "A person does not forego the income available in private practice to run for a judgeship and then find himself in the position of an administrator." The statement reflects an attitude present throughout society: Members of any profession prefer to pursue the type of activity that they feel most competent performing. Management is not the primary interest of judges or attorneys. Thus, most chief judges in Florida are apparently much more content in a traditional judicial role that involves only judicial decision making and excludes the necessity to "administer."[7]

Court clerks appear to be aware of the chief judges' disinclination to exercise fully their administrative prerogatives. While many clerks may welcome this abdication of responsibility, a sizable number in this study recognized the difficulties that ensue. For example, a recurring complaint of the court clerks was that that there are no administrative guidelines to direct their judicial activities. Among the comments reflecting this sentiment are the following: "My greatest problem is trying to find an authoritative source"; "I am continually plagued by the lack of set procedures"; and "There is a total lack of uniformity in the duties expected of me, and the procedures to be used, from one judge to the next."

The periodic rotation of chief judges in each circuit leads to an erratic form of administrative direction that is counterproductive to continuity and efficiency. Most chief judges are openly hesitant to institute broad procedural and operational reforms that will necessarily affect the activities of their colleagues and successors. Moreover, newly elected administrative judges often revise the management practices of their predecessors and thus confuse and frustrate other judicial personnel. Consequently, active and progressive management is frequently abandoned in favor of passive "crisis management" in which chief judges respond to problems but do not attempt to plan for future contingencies, and individual circuit judges thus have a relatively free hand in managing their respective judicial domains.

In addition to the natural disinclinations of chief judges toward administration, another operational aspect of this role produces negative sentiments and detracts from their willingness to assert management authority. Specifically, many chief judges commented about the unrequited nature of the position. When asked to delineate their most important administrative problems, almost the entire sample noted that conducting business with other elected officials is often a difficult and thankless task. In the words of one chief judge:

All the people I work with are elected. They want to protect their own turf. Everyone has their own extensive operations that don't directly affect the operation of the courts. When I make a decision I have to make it within the capabilities of each official to accomplish an objective, plus that person's willingness to accomplish it.

Moreover, by acting as the mediator of disputes between elected officials, the chief judges inevitably alienate the defeated party. The potential gravity of this situation is aptly illustrated by the following exchange:

Interviewer: Why is it so difficult to obtain the cooperation of the other officials in the judicial system?

Chief judge: I have a clerk, sheriff, and four county commissioners who think they're God.

Interviewer: How do you deal with them?

Chief judge: I have the patience of Job and the diplomacy of Henry Kissinger.

Clearly, the strain of coping with management pressures divests the office of chief judge of any glamor or excitement it might have once held for the enthusiastic novice. In fact, one interview was cancelled because the chief judge had unexpectedly resigned his administrative duties the preceding day.

The final factor that potentially affects the chief judges' performance of administrative duties is the degree of management ability present among the judiciary. Most judges "have not been accustomed to developing proficiency or talent in the processing of litigation."[8] Lacking formal administrative training and experience, judges frequently resist both the concept and application of management because of ignorance or misunderstanding. Judicial independence and "discreet aloofness"[9] thus take precedence over the assertion of management authority.

Some authors contend that judges are by nature poor administrators. This theory may be advanced as a partial explanation for the chief judges' inability to manage properly, but it does not account for their reluctance to make a concerted attempt. Although the depiction of judges as poor administrators may indeed be valid, there are few applicable measures to prove or refute the theory. The only indicators that are within the scope of this study are those that relate to actual performance.

The major consequence of these factors inhibiting the exercise of judicial administrative authority is that the circuits are primarily without uniform management direction. Court clerks and parochially oriented judges have assumed a large measure of administrative responsibility by default. Consequently, the traditional nexus between the court managers and the counties endures. Local political preferences and values continue to greatly influence the judicial system and contribute to the plethora of management dilemmas that preclude the success of the unification movement.

The Impact of Localism

The most conspicuous characteristic of the Florida judicial system is that no real "system" exists. Rather, the courts are fragmented into sixty-seven distinct subunits.[10] Each court clerk, in concert with his county commission, designs and supervises the judicial functions in his own county. Consequently, there are sixty-seven divergent organizational frameworks that utilize a multitude of

(1) budgetary, (2) personnel, and (3) clerical and managerial procedures. Many of the most grievous judicial maladies arise directly from the resulting incongruities.

Instead of being an isolated example, the Florida experience in these aspects of court management is perhaps representative of states in which county control over judicial operations is pronounced. For example, the National Center for State Courts conducted a study of the Maine court system in 1975.[11] The conclusions of that study bear a striking resemblance to the findings included herein. Indeed, most of the problems in the Maine courts are identical to those in Florida. This fact is particularly noteworthy when one considers that most states utilize similar administrative arranagements to those in Maine and Florida.

Budgetary Dilemmas

Local control over court budgets is often cited as a principal contributory catalyst of locally generated judicial problems.[12] The budget instrument is the most finite statement of government policy and societal values. Consequently, the persons who determine court fiscal priorities exert tremendous influence on judicial management policies. Court clerks and county commissioners often advocate locally oriented fiscal programs that ignore the broad issue of judicial exigencies. The following consequences are thus evident: Disparate levels of court financing exist between the counties, and the level of technology employed in each county is largely determined by local economic capabilities.

Domination of county government over judicial budgets has resulted in a number of underfinanced courts. Both chief judges and court clerks are apparently cognizant of this situation. For example, many chief judges noted that one or more of the counties in their districts are plagued by severe financial restrictions. Moreover, twenty-one (36.8 percent) court clerks specified that their most serious administrative problem is related to scarce resources. Inadequate space, personnel, and operating revenues have contributed to what one clerk labeled "the worst court delay this county has ever had." The gravity of this situation is illustrated by the fact that a few court clerks in smaller counties are presently forced to perform clerical duties that are normally the province of deputy clerks because no resources are available to employ additional personnel.

In addition to the large number of administrative problems that potentially arise from inadequate financing, the quality of justice may also be affected. Due to insufficient facilities, a few judges complained that they might soon be compelled to schedule informal proceedings and trials in government buildings that lack traditional courtrooms and other judicial "niceties." Moreover, many counties do not possess modern judicial facilities that are designed to expedite court business. Inadequate acoustics, lighting, and physical arrangements occasionally detract from the ability of judges to process cases adequately. The lack of modern facilities can also potentially destroy the dignity of justice and negatively influence the public perception of court activities.[13]

While courts in some counties are suffering severe financial hardships, court clerks in many other counties have been able to secure sufficient resources to operate at a profit. Monies collected from filing fees, recording fees, licensing fees, and court costs have equalled or surpassed the immediate fiscal needs of several local courts, and the clerks in these counties are often able to return substantial sums to the county commissions. Many chief judges viewed this situation as simply "the clerks' desire to please the county commissions." They stated that the courts could definitely utilize the additional resources if they were made available, but court clerks are quite conservative in their economic orientations regarding the judicial system and thus are visibly delighted when a "surplus" exists.

The absence of modern technological management aides in many counties is also partially attributable to local control of the court budget. Although some scholars contend that these reforms would be detrimental to certain social groups, the use of computers and automatic data processing in the judicial system has long been advocated by court reformers.[14] Such innovations would supposedly streamline the major functions of court administration including indexing, docketing, scheduling, jury management, general accounting, and case tracking.

However, thirty-seven (65 percent) court clerks reported that they presently do not utilize any form of sophisticated technological management equipment. One court clerk remarked that the use of computers in the court system is simply "a dream of academicians," and several clerks expressed extreme doubts that the county commissions would ever countenance the capital expenditure necessary to purchase even the most primitive "innovation." A few clerks remarked that they were forced to almost "beg" commissioners for a single tape recorder or circular file.

Although most court clerks do not possess many modern technological management aides, at the time of this study several of the larger court systems had either installed or planned to install data processing and other computerized hardware. Due to the fact that thirty-nine of the counties have populations of 50,000 or below, their investing large amounts of capital in computer systems may be an unreasonable expectation when their tax bases are so restricted. However, computerization by *region* is a viable alternative, but one that is impossible to implement without centralization of responsibility and funding sources.

The lack of modernized judicial equipment has resulted in the continued use of archaic clerical techniques. For example, in more than one rural county the deputy clerks continue to make multiple handwritten entries in docket books just as their predecessors were doing one hundred years before. Several court clerks require their deputies to type copies of documents that could very easily be microfilmed or photocopied. Moreover, there is a marked lack of uniformity in the methods used to store records. Looseleaf dockets, bound dockets, index cards and index files, separate dockets for civil and criminal cases and bound dockets for both types of cases all exist.[15]

Present budgetary arrangements indicate that these and other problems, which are largely the result of inadequate funding levels, will continue. Most judges are conservative and consequently are not inclined to actively lobby for additional resources from legislative bodies.[16] The ability of judges to lobby for appropriations, even if they are so inclined, is limited by the fragmented nature of budget preparation within the counties. Budget preparation within the court system is so disjointed and irregular that using expenditure and accounting figures for control or planning—the major functions of the budgetary process—is next to impossible. Court clerks, judges, and county commissions all have divergent opinions regarding the fiscal requirements of the courts. This situation is aggravated by the fact that in multi-county circuits the judges themselves often disagree about budget priorities. Thus, county commissions and clerks both receive varying suggestions from the judiciary. Because no formal mechanism exists to enable the judges to confer with court clerks and county commissioners in order to provide explanations and justifications for proposed budgets, a vast number of budget proposals result from the chief judges' failure to consolidate fiscal responsibility in one office. County clerks and/or county commissions thus are given the initial responsibility for evaluating budget proposals and the judiciary thus assumes a relatively impotent role in the administration of its budget.[17]

The only practical criteria available to evaluate funding requests is the previous year's budget. Although the use of this incremental style of budgeting is perceived by many authorities as being functional,[18] the rapid increase in litigation throughout the state indicates that such a technique is hardly adequate when applied to the judicial system. Moreover, the political and economic predispositions of court clerks would necessarily discourage advocacy of large increases in judicial appropriations. The clerks are overwhelmingly conservative and thus would be disinclined to seek large budgets as the judges.

Although several chief judges in this study blamed parsimonious county commissions and clerks for the current financial plight of the courts, local revenues are so exiguous that many counties are barely able to maintain present funding levels. Reliance upon local funding forces the judiciary to "join the unhappy competition for the inadequate revenues of local property taxes."[19] The rapid expansion of judicial needs has placed obligations on counties that they are poorly equipped to meet in light of declining tax bases. Moreover, the counties are predictably reluctant to make financial commitments for major capital outlays when no authority within the judicial system can prognosticate future requirements of the courts.[20] Adequate estimates of judicial needs are also hindered by inconsistent standards as to what expenses will be charged to the courts. It is often unreasonable to expect impecunious counties to appropriate large sums of money to the courts when they cannot clearly define their needs.[21]

The monetary difficulties of the court system have been exacerbated by the advent of Article V, which has placed heavy additional burdens on the counties in regard to reorganization expenses and stringent new rules of criminal procedure.[22] The counties have been compelled to provide funding and space for court functions that were previously the purview of large self-supporting special courts. Moreover, clerks of the courts abolished by Article V have been statutorially designated "deputy clerks of the circuit courts."[23] Whereas these personnel had previously been paid out of revenues collected by their respective courts, their salaries are now the responsibility of the counties. Since the state government presently receives an increased proportion of revenues collected by courts, local financial resources have been further taxed by increasing personnel expenditures. According to the Staff of the Joint Select Committee on Judicial Personnel, the situation is extremely grave because the abolition of special courts "requires the counties to assume added expenses, but denies them the revenues these courts formerly generated."[24]

Further, under authority of Article V, the Florida Rules of Criminal Procedure allow every person accused of a crime to demand a trial within sixty days.[25] This provision obviously places an additional burden on court resources, since most courts have been forced to employ supplemental personnel to insure that no criminal processing exceeds the limit. Moreover, a variety of procedural refinements have been necessitated by this requirement. For example, since state attorneys may seek exceptions to the sixty-day provision, in some larger counties an administrative review process has been established to evaluate the merits of continuance requests.

The state government has recently assumed a larger percentage of the increased costs induced by Article V; yet most costs are still borne by the counties. State funds account for approximately 35 percent of all judicial expenditures.[26] While several counties at one time received state appropriations to employ additional personnel, this program was discontinued. Consequently, the state government does not presently contribute any appreciable resources to finance reorganization. Both the chief judges and court clerks appear to be bitter about the unwillingness of the state government to assume a larger proportion of court expenses. The aspect that clearly perturbs the court managers most is the failure of the state to provide replacements for those judges who retire or who are absent because of illness. This sentiment is particularly pronounced among chief judges and court executive assistants: Nine (56.3 percent) judges and five (35.7 percent) court executives specifically mentioned that a shortage of judges is one of their most severe problems. Moreover, the influx of Law Enforcement Assistance Administration grants to local police forces has resulted in greatly expanded arrests and thus larger numbers of criminal prosecutions. Plagued by inadequate funds and absent judges, several circuits have encountered serious problems in conforming to the sixty-day trial requirement. In at least two circuits chief judges have been forced to transfer civil court judges into the criminal divisions in order to keep dockets current.

Process Dilemmas

The second major management dilemma that may be directly attributed to local influence in the judicial system is the lack of uniformity in forms and procedures utilized among the counties. Although a large proportion of judicial legal forms and procedures are specifically delineated by statute and Supreme Court Rules, the court clerks' application of these state guidelines has been termed "lackadaisical,"[27] and in the areas where state law is vague or nonexistent regarding forms and procedures, local court clerks have created their own individualized practices. A recent study conducted under the auspices of the Office of State Courts Administrator revealed a large number of startling facts in this regard: "Clerks presently utilize over sixteen thousand different versions of like forms. Forms are created with insufficient consideration given to their design, utility, or cost." [28] The report also states that inconsistent forms and procedures create inconsistencies in the ways cases are handled.[29]

A corresponding variation in filing procedures employed among the clerks' offices places burdens on both attorneys practicing in more than one county and the public conducting business in more than one county. The variations in procedures have been so pronounced that the legal community has advocated complete obligatory standardization of judicial procedures. The Court Management Seminars were instituted partially to systematize procedures by educating the court clerks about the most practical and economic methods of performing their functions. Nevertheless, the Staff of the Joint Select Committee on Judicial Personnel reports that several court clerks have failed to institute even the most crucial aspects of recent procedural reforms.[30] Moreover, many clerks have reputedly "misinterpreted statutes" in so many ways that even the circuit judges are occasionally bewildered by the resulting variations in procedures and practices.[31]

Of the hundreds of procedural variations occurring within the Florida judicial system, perhaps the most blatant examples appear in the areas of exhibits, minute books, and summonses. Presently each court clerk establishes whatever procedures he deems appropriate in processing and disposing of exhibits. "Each clerk does as he thinks best, which means that sometimes more is being done than necessary and less is being done in some situations than should be."[32] While some clerks retain possession of exhibits for inordinate amounts of time, others have been known to dispose of essential properties before their usefulness has expired.[33]

Because the statutes are imprecise regarding procedural standards for "keeping the minutes," each judge, clerk, and deputy clerk has a different concept of what information and format is pertinent in these records. In some counties minutes are kept for both circuit and county court proceedings, while in several counties no minutes at all or only record abbreviated versions are kept. Thus, attorneys and judges are never certain of the location or nature of official court records.[34]

The summons procedures utilized by court clerks continue this trend of inconsistency. In some counties each arrestee is automatically advised about the location and date of his trial during the booking process. Conversely, a number of other counties either require the sheriff to deliver the summons personally, or it is forwarded by certified mail. Consequently, many arrestees released on recognizance are never contacted due to the inability of the clerks and sheriffs to locate them.[35]

When the negative effects of the three examples of procedural variation are multiplied by the tremendous number of other irregularities present in the system, the depth of the problems created by local control becomes apparent. The extent to which local control of court administration can potentially inhibit proper administration is aptly illustrated in the following account. Within the past five years, Broward, Orange, and Hillsborough Counties instituted special procedures to collect support payments. They established a unique agency within the clerks' offices to insure that support payments are made on time and to monitor the receiving family in order to determine whether the funds are being utilized beneficially. Despite the recognized advantages to be gained by such an arrangement, no other county has yet implemented a similar plan. The fragmentation of administrative authority hinders transporting novel solutions to judicial problems across county boundaries.[36]

Personnel Dilemmas

The impact of localism is even more significant in the area of personnel administration than it is in budgetary or procedural matters. As Roscoe Pound stated early in the history of American judicial reform: "The judiciary is the only great agency of government which is habitually given no control over its clerical force. Even the pettiest agency has much more control than the average court."[37] Court staffs perform a variety of functions that are prerequisites for effective administration of the judicial system. Yet all recording, processing, scheduling, and filing duties are generally performed by subordinate personnel who are responsible to a person who is not directly accountable to the court.

The court clerks in Florida exercise almost dictatorial control over the administration of support personnel within the judicial system. Under Article V chief judges have the authority to establish whatever personnel requirements and procedures they desire, but no judge has actually attempted to exercise it. Each clerk independently recruits, selects, trains, evaluates, and compensates his deputy clerks according to locally derived standards, and this situation has resulted in numerous inconsistencies and inefficiencies that inhibit effective court management and lead to serious management dilemmas.

The most widely noted criticism of local control over court personnel is that such an arrangement inevitably leads to political patronage.[38] Presumably, independently elected court clerks repay political debts by utilizing a "spoils system" form of personnel administration. Although there appears to be no widespread occurrence of this phenomenon in Florida, there are a few indications that political considerations do affect employment practices. For example, three clerks in this study (5.3 percent) report that the party affiliation of prospective employees is an important criteria in the recruitment process. While this percentage is quite small, the mere fact that three persons are willing to admit to such priorities is considered noteworthy. Moreover, the political nature of deputy clerks' positions is exemplified by the fact that in several counties the turnover rate of the court clerks' staffs is nearly 100 percent whenever a new incumbent assumes office. As a result, many deputies expressed apprehension that they may lose their jobs if a new clerk is elected.

Regardless of political considerations, the recruitment processes utilized by court clerks are often insufficient to assure an adequate supply of competent judicial manpower. Only a few counties have instituted formal recruitment procedures that resemble civil service practices. The remaining clerks use varying mixtures of formal and informal criteria; for example, most clerks hire any person who is able to type and who has acquired a high school diploma. In many counties the candidates are required to complete a simple aptitude test successfully. However, the general laxity in employment standards is attested to by the following statement of one clerk: "Most of us hire anyone who 'looks' alright [sic]." By his own admission, one court clerk employed a "man off the street" to assume his judicial functions. The person who was hired had been a school teacher with presumably no knowledge of and absolutely no experience relating to the courts.

The informality present in recruitment practices recurs in the training that deputy clerks are required to undergo. Only a small percentage of the clerks have established any type of formalized training program. A few counties have recently employed training officers to supervise the instruction of new employees, but the persons who occupy these positions are generally inexperienced with court procedures and thus have been compelled to develop expertise in the field independently. Several clerks reported that they "move the deputy clerks around" into every possible position so that all personnel will acquire the "flavor" of the office. However, this type of training procedure would only seem to be beneficial in instances where one deputy is absent and a replacement is needed.

A majority of deputy clerks thus appear to receive only on-the-job training. Consequently, many learn their duties from personnel who already occupy similar positions within the court. This training technique is potentially hazardous because it increases the opportunity for incorrect and/or inefficient clerical practices to be transferred from one employee to another. The slogan "we've always done it this way" appears to be used to legitimize and rationalize practices that have not been formally evaluated according to efficiency criteria.

A sizable number of other deputy clerks apparently do not even receive the simple luxury of being "broken in" by a colleague. Several court clerks reported that the only training their deputies receive consists of "reading the section of the *Florida Statutes* that deals with the duties of Clerks of Court." Any employee who has received this inadequate level of instruction clearly must rely upon actual experience to develop competence in the position.

The lack of standardized recruitment and training practices utilized by most court clerks thus indicates that the competence level of deputy clerks employed throughout the state is not entirely adequate. Moreover, a number of other inconsistencies exist in working conditions that frustrate many courts' attempts to employ and retain competent personnel. For example, the average initial salary of deputy clerks is approximately $5,200 annually. Clerks in rural counties with large urban neighbors reported that they have experienced difficulties in retaining qualified deputies. Small counties cannot afford to pay their deputies salaries comparable to those available in private business or in clerks' offices situated in more wealthy areas. "As soon as I get a good clerk trained, they hire him away" is a common complaint.[39]

In addition to inadequate salaries, the fringe benefits available to court personnel are inconsistent among the clerks' offices and do not generally equal those received for comparable work in other occupations. For example, some counties offer free hospitalization and life insurance to their personnel, while minimum retirement benefits and workmen's compensation are the only benefits available in many of the remaining counties.[40] A great deal of friction and confusion is created by the fact that disparities exist in the number of holidays various counties recognize:

It isn't hard to imagine the confusion among court workers who talk to each other by phone every day and transfer cases back and forth when they find that some counties give as many as thirteen holidays while others give as few as six. And except for Christmas, those holidays that are recognized seem to coincide by freakest chance.[41]

A logical consequence of disparate personnel procedures is that deputy clerks in many counties are slow to develop either expertise or professional orientations toward their positions. Chief judges are obviously cognizant of this situation. For example, several judges remarked that court operations could be performed with much less confusion and inefficiency if deputy clerks were properly trained. One judge offered the following account in order to emphasize his argument for improved personnel standards: "We had one deputy clerk who was a 'winner.' Occasionally she would encounter a case which she didn't understand, or didn't know what to do with. What do you think she did? She filed them [sic] away!" Although this example is obviously extreme, the employees' awareness of the importance of their judicial tasks is clearly considered by some judges to be at an extremely low level.

Many of the most critical management dilemmas arise from undersupervision of deputy clerks. All clerical duties relating to recording and case processing are ostensibly the most important judicial functions of court clerks; yet deputy clerks often perform these tasks with little or no guidance. Many county-oriented responsibilities consume a large proportion of the court clerks' working day, and they cannot be expected to devote their full attention to court administration when they must also be attentive to the needs of the county commission. Primarily as a result of county responsibilities, thirty-three clerks (57.9 percent) reported that their judicial functions are delegated to subordinate personnel. Consequently, many deputy clerks are often "on their own" in performing court duties. As one deputy clerk stated: "The clerk has no idea of what's going on. He really does not understand the workings of the court. This really isn't surprising, because he's never here long enough to know what any of us are doing."

Of similar significance is the fact that judges and court administrators reported that they are extremely hesitant to supervise and/or instruct deputy clerks. Only two chief judges stated that an "accepted practice" in their circuits is for judges to supervise or instruct deputies. Most clerks are clearly defensive about their assistants and object to any perceived incursions into their domains. For example, a chief judge in one circuit reported that when the court clerk discovered the court executive assistant in a neighboring circuit was attempting to correct several improper practices being followed by local deputy clerks, a serious altercation ensued. The court executive assistant has now been ordered "never to show his face in the clerk's office."

Perhaps the most serious consequence of undersupervision is that the deputy clerks are often ignorant of procedural and clerical requirements that emanate from the Florida Supreme Court or the state legislature. The following comments of deputy clerks signify the gravity of this situation: "None of the other court employees ever are informed about statute changes, and when they are they refuse to do anything about it"; "The clerk never communicates new procedures. I even have to give him newspaper clippings to let him know about changes"; "No one ever knows what duties or procedures to follow for filing claims and actions"; and "My biggest problem is maintaining high morale among the deputies. It's very frustrating to never know whether you're doing something right or not." As these statements indicate, many court clerks are apparently failing to provide their subordinates with information that is essential for the efficient administration of their courts.

Much of the discrepancy among procedures utilized in the various clerks' offices thus originates with the deputy clerks. Because they are often not adequately supervised, these personnel have continued to perform their duties in a style that is inefficient and obsolete. The propensity of any functionary in the bureaucracy to resist change and to strive to retain the status quo is widely recognized. Consequently, traditional modes of operation cannot be replaced by modernistic and innovative operational procedures until forceful management authority is exercised by court clerks. However, most clerks are clearly not energetic advocates of reform; they are as susceptible to the inertia of traditionalism as are the deputies. The resulting combination of habit and undersupervision of subordinates dictates that renovated management procedures will not be readily implemented.

Fragmented Administrative Authority

A central theme of the preceding discussion is that the chief judges' reluctance to assume firm administrative control over their circuits enables local officials to exercise enormous discretionary powers in managing the judicial structure. A realistic appraisal of the current constitutional status of court clerks, chief judges, and the judicial system in general indicates that fragmentation is a natural outgrowth of an illogical distribution of judicial administrative authority. Despite the fact that the judiciary has ostensibly been granted control over its own management destiny, several aspects of state law tend to disperse the judges' authority and thus allow other political entities to establish court management priorities. Specifically, the two characteristics of the present system of court management that are most pertinent in explaining this phenomenon are: (1) local control over the courts' budgets, and (2) legislative and executive provisions governing judicial activity.

Local Budget Control

The greatest single hindrance to judicial unification in Florida is the system of locally financed courts. The existing system of court financing prohibits the actual execution of ultimate administrative authority and thus prevents any movement toward uniformity in administration. Because chief judges must rely upon court clerks for monetary supports, a lack of clarity exists between the administrative roles of the court managers. The chief judges must depend upon court clerks for implementation of the judicial policy, "but their lack of direct influence on the clerks' operating revenues severely restricts their authority to coordinate or manage the activities those revenues finance."[42] Consequently, chief judges have been compelled to maintain traditional political relationships with court clerks in order to assure the continued funding and policy implementation "cooperation" of local officials.

A further consequence of this system of local budgetary control is that court clerks possess an extensive amount of political "clout" and are often able to arbitrarily resist the supervision of court authority. Although the incidence of this behavior is rare, a few examples are notable. A few judges commented that, on occasion, court clerks would refuse to comply with a court mandate. A court clerk reported that his chief judge had occasionally attempted to "use me as his personal secretary," and consequently he instructed his own secretary that he is "no longer available to the chief judge." Perhaps the most dramatic instance of court clerks' recalcitrance in responding to judicial demands occurred in Jacksonville in 1975. A county judge ordered a court clerk to sign an order for him, and the clerk steadfastly refused, even under the threat of a contempt decree. During the debate that followed, the judge accused the clerk in open court of "constantly making unilateral decisions and letting his clerks defy orders of the court."[43] The court clerk did not relent in his refusal to comply to the judge's wishes.

In addition to affecting the relationship between judges and clerks, local budgetary control has also severely restricted state-wide judicial policy options. Although there are statutory requirements that each clerk report his budget to various state judicial and executive officials, the budgeting systems among the counties are so diverse that it is virtually impossible for anyone to draw conclusions or to make generalizations on the information being reported.[44]

This phenomenon recurs in the areas of personnel and general administration. The supreme court and state legislature are rigidly limited in enacting state-wide judicial policies affecting either of these areas. Before any new policy is enacted, the state government must necessarily appraise the ability of each county to conform to the dictate. Because funding levels and administrative practices and procedures vary so widely among the counties, a state requirement for uniformity in any single area may conceivably surpass the abilities of many counties to comply.

As a result of these factors, it is entirely unreasonable to expect any sole agency or individual to assume total administrative authority and responsibility over the judicial system. The existence of numerous distinct court organizations diffuses accountability to a practically irreducible level.[45] Moreover, the formulation and execution of any pragmatic policy requires that comprehensive planning precede legislative action. However, it is debatable that such planning can occur in a system in which no authority can predict the consequences of an action. Under the present structure, conformity to hierarchically imposed laws and rules depends upon the willingness and ability of the various court managers to comply. If a local official decides to ignore the dictates of state agencies, few politically feasible devices are available to judicial authorities to force cooperation.

Legislative and Executive Controls

The fragmentation of administrative authority that is endemic to Florida's judicial system may also be traced to a source completely external to the courts.

Article II, Section 3 of the Florida Constitution states: "There shall be three equal and coordinate branches of government, none of which shall exercise powers appertaining to the others." Therefore, the separation of powers doctrine is clearly embodied in state law. However, existing legislation obscures the issue of administrative authority with respect to the courts. For example, there is legislation that characterizes the judiciary as a state agency, or a unit of the executive branch, for purposes of administration.[46] In addition, existing legislation[47] requires the judiciary to submit its budgets to the governor for his review and modification and for incorporation into the total state budget. This power of prior review grants to the executive and legislative branches the responsibility for interpreting policy and for establishing priorities within the judicial system.[48]

The current legal status of the Florida judicial system is thus extremely confused. The constitutional and statutory provisions that govern Florida's courts place the judicial bureaucracy in a position of "double administrative accountability."[49] Numerous facets of court management in Florida are subject to the review and approval of external authorities. Thus, the chief justice is placed in the position of a relatively impotent administrator whose decisions are directed and circumscribed by legislative and executive authorities alike, and the absence of unified and authoritative direction results in a corresponding management vacuum at the circuit and county court levels. Crisis management becomes the norm, and the court management "system" is one of maintenance, not direction.

The role of the state legislature in judicial affairs represents more than simply a fundamental restraint on court administrative authority. Legislative enactments govern a wide range of judicial activity. For example, statutes define court jurisdiction,[50] acceptable standards for terms of court[51] and summary procedures,[52] and detailed procedures to be followed under such laws as the landlord-tenant act,[53] and the decriminalization of traffic offenses act.[54] Moreover, a tremendous number of statutory provisions address almost every aspect of judicial administration. Court clerks and judges are thus continually plagued by new procedural and administrative guidelines established with little prior consultation and without a realistic determination of the impact they exert on court management.

Legislative involvement in court administration is both illogical and inefficient for a number of reasons. In an effort to retain their "independence," most judges are reluctant to enter the political arena. Thus, communication between the legislative and executive branches is quite exiguous and ineffective. The legislature is therefore often poorly informed about the needs and problems of the court system. Moreover, since the legislature is an institution with a constantly changing membership, there is little opportunity to construct or supervise interminable reform programs. Finally, legislators are unlikely to consider court reforms as a major priority because public knowledge and concern regarding the courts is generally minimal.[55] Therefore, the legislature can hardly be expected to, of its own volition, make substantial efforts toward improving the conditions of the judiciary simply because the courts request it to do so.

The consequences of legislative involvement in court administration are clearly evident in court clerks' responses to questions regarding their most important problems. Ten clerks (31.6 percent adjusted frequency) specifically list "legislative controls" as their most pressing administrative dilemma. Their comments generally reflect the opinion that state directives are "too numerous," "unreasonable," and "inconsistent." Among the most descriptive comments are the following: "The legislature has a complete lack of understanding in passing laws as to the problems created in carrying them out"; "In order to keep up with state enactments I spend all my time improvising"; and "Trying to satisfy contradictory requirements from the Legislature, as well as keeping up with all the red tape, is a tremendous chore." According to the Office of State Courts Administrator, "Clerks are hampered in efficiently carrying out their responsibilities by laws which specify certain record creation and maintenance practices, by forms and procedures imposed outside their jursidction and by unrealistic records scheduling and disposal requirements."[56] Statutes are regarded as unsuitable guidelines for clerks because inconsistencies, voids, unclear meanings, and mistaken interpretations result.[57]

Examples of such shortcomings abound. Sections 111.09, 267.051 (7) and (8) of the *Florida Statutes* control the retention and disposition of records. Although these statutes provide for the destruction of some records after a specific period of time, they also require that records having continued value be preserved. Because the law is extremely vague as to what records belong in each category, court clerks have developed their own criteria for determining which documents will be retained. This procedure has resulted in tremendous discrepancies among the counties. While a few clerks attempt to dispose of nonessential records, most are presently inundated by millions of documents that are often extremely dated.[58]

A startling amount of discrepancy and uncertainty also exists among statutory provisions governing dockets. As with most state guidelines relating to the courts, the terminology used to "direct" the court clerks in docketing procedures is so vague that individual county interpretation predominates. The term *docket* is defined in over twenty different ways throughout the statutes. Some examples are: fee docket, execution docket, court docket, bench docket, trial docket, progress docket, motion docket, judgment docket, default docket, will docket, and clerk's docket.[59] Therefore, many of the inconsistent and inefficient administrative procedures utilized by various court clerks can be at least partially attributed to inadequate legislative provisions.

From a realistic perspective, legislative and executive involvement in court administration inhibits effective judicial control and decelerates reform. Because many court management policies are established in other branches of government, the conception of a judicial system as "just another state agency"[60] is accentuated and prolonged. The court system has not been allowed to function as an independent branch of government; it is granted even less control over its administrative and policy processes than are most other government organizations. Consequently, the judiciary has been unable to develop into an effective force for change.[61]

Summary

Article V was intended by its authors to unify and coordinate Florida's judicial system. However, the impact of local influence and the accompanying independence of court clerks has resulted in management irregularities that indicate the aspirations of reformers have not yet been realized. Judicial efficiency and "manageability" have sustained a severe blow from the perpetuance of fragmentation. Disparate budgetary, procedural, and personnel policies have resulted in serious management dilemmas. Existing relationships between the courts and other political entities prevent the judiciary from acquiring preeminent control over its own destiny. Reliance upon local political entities for financial support and upon other branches of government for management policies tends to increase fragmentation in all spheres of judicial activity and indicates that present management irregularities will persist.

These findings should serve as a warning to reformers in other states. According to a study by Larry C. Berkson, Florida's court system is more "unified" than those in approximately thirty-five other states.[62] Other studies by James A. Gazell indicate that the personnel practices and general administrative makeup of the Florida system are relatively typical of transitional systems.[63] Other researchers are just now beginning to thoroughly analyze the effects of fragmentation on lower court administration in the fifty states.

Unfortunately, the findings in future studies are likely to approximate the ones in this analysis. For example, the court clerk in Orange County, California, had many of his judicial functions taken away from him during the summer of 1977. The judges of the superior court voted to take this action due to administrative inefficiencies, poor morale among deputy clerks, inadequate training of support personnel, and the fact that the clerk "was more interested in presenting a low budget to the Board of Supervisors than in 'going to bat' for legitimate needs."[64] Such reports are surfacing more frequently and potentially represent only the proverbial "tip of the iceberg."

Obviously, the only technique that apparently will insure consistent management in reformed states is to give the judicial branch control over its own resources and personnel. Uniformity in any organization is contingent upon cohesive administrative direction from a group of managers who possess similar conceptions of organizational goals and who have the capacity to channel organizational resources toward those objectives. The subsequent chapter examines various methods that may conceivably be utilized to transform the judicial branch of government into a viable modernizing force.

4

Reforming the Judicial System

Because of their small size and consistent mission relative to other governmental agencies, judicial systems are potentially capable of becoming extremely "businesslike" public organizations.[1] Administrative effectiveness, if not efficiency, is a prerequisite to the ultimate attainment of justice.[2] However, the previous discussion reveals that Article V has failed to provide several fundamental requirements that necessarily precede efficiency. The most serious management dilemmas arise from a pronounced absence of definitive administrative authority. Florida's court managers are plagued by overlapping and poorly defined responsibilities. Moreover, the powers that these personnel do possess are often granted without adequate consideration of the managers' potential ability to operationalize them. For example, chief judges are responsible for the administrative direction of their circuits; yet they exercise almost no control over the personnel who implement management policies.

As a consequence of the division of administrative authority, the various court managers do not constitute cohesive leadership. Each distinct group of managers, already divided by differing selection procedures, reward systems, and "attentive publics," possesses its own individual conception of judicial goals. Chief judges generally adhere to an organizational goal that is often expressed in terms of "individual justice in individual cases." Conversely, court clerks are primarily concerned with locally oriented goals involving fiscal and political considerations. As might be expected in any organization hampered by diffused responsibility and conflicting goals, Florida's courts are burdened by a critical lack of administrative direction that prevents efficient management.

The present chapter examines various remedies to the management irregularities and inefficiencies that have been generated by the fragmented nature of judicial authority. Primary emphasis is placed on administrative aspects of court operations such as the organizational roles of court managers and political and economic reforms designed to enforce judicial responsibility. Technical and legal questions involving such topics as substantive law reform,[3] expedited procedures,[4] settlement conferences,[5] and accelerated appeals have been excluded due to their perceived secondary importance to purely administrative matters. Presumably the numerous techniques that have been suggested by court reformers as possible solutions to court delay and inefficiency cannot be effectively implemented until the more immediate question of judicial responsibility is resolved.

Redefining the Roles of Court Managers

In order to manage their organizations consistently and effectively, judicial administrators must possess power and authority that is commensurate with their responsibility.[6] According to Arthur D. Larson, "There is wide agreement among scholars, laymen, and government officials that the principal problems of the public bureaucracy today are not the traditional ones of securing competence and efficiency, but those of insuring responsibility."[7] Although Article V clearly vests authority and responsibility in chief judges, neither concept is well developed within the court system. Due to their inability and/or unwillingness to utilize their constitutional authority, the chief judges have not availed themselves of a valuable organizational asset that could conceivably succor accelerated reform. Moreover, the diffused nature of judicial responsibility has obscured management roles to the point that few court managers clearly comprehend the functions expected of them. Consequently, the most immediate requirement for management efficiency and consistency within the judicial system is a clarified role definition for each of the three groups of court managers.

Chief Judges

Compared to other groups of court managers, the roles of the chief judges are relatively well-defined by statute, supreme court rule, and constitutional provisions. Article V leaves no doubt that chief judges are intended to assume administrative control over their respective circuits. However, statutory ambiguities and deficiencies in the realm of explicit delineations of judicial functions have enabled chief judges to evade this role definition. Chapter 43.26 of the *Florida Statutes* contains the most concise delineation of the chief judges' authority and duties. The statute is insufficient in two areas: It does not *require* administrative judges to perform their functions, and it excludes a large number of powers that judges must possess in order to be effective managers. For example, while presiding judges are granted authority to assign clerks and to supervise dockets and calendars, no substantive powers are granted in the policy areas of budgeting, personnel administration, or clerical supervision. In fact, the duties listed in the statute do not vary significantly from the functions chief judges performed prior to the adoption of Article V.

In addition, the Florida Supreme Court, through the Office of State Courts Administrator, has been somewhat negligent in utilizing its rule-making and administrative authority to supervise trial courts and thereby provide chief judges with assistance. For example, the state administrative office does not have the authority to require trial courts to provide it with budget information, to establish personnel qualifications for support personnel, or to approve requisitions.[8] Thus, because no authoritative source has established specific criteria to direct the judges' administrative behavior, most have not attempted ·to manage any judicial activities other than those that their predecessors performed prior to reform.

Specifying the Judges' Responsibilities. In order to assure consistent and forceful administration by the chief judges, their requisite functions and duties must necessarily be legitimized by supreme court rule. Only through an elaborate delineation of administrative duties can these personnel be expected to exercise ultimate management authority. Moreover, such an inventory of functions is a prerequisite to the firm establishment of administrative responsibility in the chief judges' offices. Most bureaucracies explicitly define the jurisdiction and functions of each person in the hierarchy in order to control their activities and to insure maximum effort. Through this mechanism the organization determines responsibility for its goals. Much of the management vacuum present in the judicial system may be directly attributed to its failure to adhere to this basic organizational tenet.

Therefore, the Florida Supreme Court should not only establish a finite management system to be followed by chief judges, but should also institute control mechanisms to insure that the unified administrative policies are implemented. While the presiding judges of each circuit should establish local administrative policy, any rules and procedures that are formulated must necessarily be designed to conform to guidelines drafted by the Chief Justice of the Florida Supreme Court.[9] Through this mechanism continuity in rule application and procedures is partially assured; yet provisions are made for local contingencies that require "unusual treatment."[10] Although this general management arrangement presently exists within Florida's judicial system, legal mechanisms are required to persuade chief judges to exercise the authority they have possessed since 1972.

Administrative judges are required to confront the same leadership issues that managers in other organizations face. Among executive functions that chief judges must be convinced to undertake are the following: setting output goals; monitoring progress toward the output goals; establishing and maintaining unity of command; organizing the judicial structure in a functional manner; instituting management control systems; and supervising the "housekeeping" operations such as recruitment, training, and evaluation of judicial support personnel.[11] Numerous legal authorities and judicial reform commissions have analyzed and evaluated the requisite powers that must be specifically granted to chief judges in order to insure their cooperation in performing these functions. The only consensus that arises from these reform proposals is that the pattern of administrative functions should be clearly established and management authority and responsibility should be clearly vested in judicial officers. By vesting all local administrative authority in one office, the number of decision points and opposing goals present within judicial systems will be reduced. Achievement of this goal is contingent upon two major powers that chief judges have yet to be granted: (1) control over judicial and quasi-judicial support personnel, and (2) control over the judicial budget.

In order to obtain any semblance of uniformity or continuity among the circuits, chief judges must be accorded legitimate control over support personnel. For the purposes of this study, "support personnel" are composed of what James A. Gazell terms "technical" employees.[12] Bailiffs, clerks, deputy clerks, court reporters, court librarians, and the like should have solely "judicial" responsibilities that are subject to court control. The vast number of other "professional"[13] personnel who service the courts, such as diversion employees and probation officers, are excluded.

No organization can expect to function adequately when it cannot directly control the actions of its employees. Personnel who are responsible to political entities outside of the judicial system have no apparent allegiance to the courts and have few incentives to perform their functions efficiently.[14] Consequently, organizational rationality requires that presiding judges possess ultimate power to recruit, remove, compensate, train, and evaluate all judicial and support employees.

A corresponding requirement for judicial administrative efficacy is that chief judges assume partial operational direction of the functions and duties performed by all personnel they supervise. Requisite to gaining the competence required to manage support personnel effectively, as is generally assumed, administrators must be at least tangentially involved in the daily operation of the organization. Efficient administration thus requires that presiding judges develop awareness of the problems and responsibilities of those personnel performing recording, filing, and general office management functions. While no judge can be expected to develop expertise in the plethora of support activities, a modicum of knowledge about such functions is necessary for coordination and control of the court organization. This function could easily be operationalized through the circuit court administrators' offices. In larger circuits requiring judges to abandon their "judging" duties during their tenure as administrative officers may be advisable. Establishment of a judicial department personnel system has also been advocated by several reform commissions as a partial solution to the courts' need to control and supervise judicial employees. Such a mechanism would lighten the personnel responsibilities of presiding judges by performing all recruitment, training, and evaluation functions, yet would enable the judiciary to maintain control over these aspects of the court bureaucracy.

The last major group of responsibilities that chief judges need to acquire are those involving fiscal matters. According to Standard 9.2(5) of the National Advisory Commission on Criminal Justice Standards and Goals, "The presiding judge must have responsibility for accounts and auditing as well as procurement and disbursing. He should also prepare the court's proposed annual budget."[15]

This power, more than any other, will enable the judges to coordinate and manage the judicial system effectively. Without budgetary control chief judges are "mere figureheads limited to the clerical duties of assigning judges to various departments."[16] The budget instrument is an integrating and coordinating mechanism that enables administrators to plan for future contingencies and to consolidate their authority. Moreover, situating total circuit fiscal control in one office reduces the possibility that other political entities in the courts' environment can unduly influence the judicial policy-making process. Much of the chief judges' failure to exercise the authority granted to them in Article V, Section 2(d) is directly related to their inability to control operating revenues. Judicial independence and accountability has been severely eroded by the fiscal responsibilities of local officials. Consequently, active administrative participation by the chief judges may be promoted by court budget control.

Increased judicial input into the budgetary process is also viewed as a crucial factor in inducing chief judges to assert more actively the powers that have already been granted to them by statutes and supreme court rules. As has been previously stated, a "crisis management" orientation prevails among most judges. Their lack of influence in personnel and budgetary matters has resulted in an impotent judiciary that often fails to utilize available rule-making power. Due to their inability either to predict the amount of resources to be allocated in the future or to control the actions of support personnel, chief judges have been inactive administrators. However, upon gaining control over total judicial operations, chief judges will have the opportunity to discover and treat potential problems before they become serious detriments to the organization. Moreover, improved judicial functioning should result from the judges' increasing ability to evaluate performance and to recommend and independently implement changes in the organization and operation of the courts.[17]

Developing Assertive Administrators. Placing such an enormous amount of responsibility in a central position does not necessarily insure proper administration. In fact, the aspects of court administration that inhibit the chief judges' exercise of administrative authority are only partially nullified by vesting personnel and budgetary responsibilities in their offices. Whether or not judicial executives will voluntarily utilize their powers is dependent upon the following factors: the administrative ability of chief judges; the strength of traditional political relationships; and the level of interference from other court managers and local political entities.

It is a truism that responsible leadership requires a merging of authority and ability. Regardless of the amount of power granted to judicial executives, proper administration depends upon their ability and competence to utilize their authority in a constructive manner. However, most chief judges, by their own admission, are totally lacking in administrative expertise or training.[18] The only formal training program for circuit judges in Florida offers little more than seminars in pleadings, motions, discovery, and contempt proceedings. According to Maurice Rosenberg, "At the top of any list of factors determining a court's effectiveness is the judge himself."[19] The only way to insure effective administrative judges is by "giving judges now on the bench a program of advanced courses on both the substance and administration of their work."[20] Numerous other authorities have noted that a license to practice law does not equip a judge to administer complex organizations. The legal community has now recognized the absurdity of this situation, and presently all but four states provide some type of continuing education program for their judges.[21] In many states these programs are mandatory for all new judges, lay judges, and/or sitting judges.[22] The establishment of a similar instructional program in Florida is perceived by most authorities as being crucial in both enhancing the administrative ability of chief judges and in increasing their willingness to assume management responsibility. Such a plan is currently being considered by the Florida Supreme Court.[23]

Another aspect of the chief judges' administrative role that requires radical alteration is the present system of rotating their terms of office every two years. The establishment of an independently administered judicial branch requires stability at the policy-making level. Judicial executives should serve minimum terms of four years or more.[24] Judges beginning such lengthy tenure will be more inclined to institute comprehensive administrative programs. Four-year terms in office will provide chief judges with adequate opportunity to experiment and to develop expertise, in addition to reducing their apprehension that forceful management will either "tie the hands" of succeeding judges or alienate their colleagues.

An element of the present system that should be retained is the method of selecting chief judges by the vote of their peers. Such a procedure is beneficial in solidifying the judicial executives' administrative positions. Chief judges who are elected by their colleagues are in "a natural position to ask for and receive cooperation."[25] In addition, local election of chief judges will avoid the impression that the central state administration is attempting to "dictate policy" to local jurisdictions. This fact should partially reassure opponents of increased state control and thus expedite the progress of reform. However, as should be noted, while local judges might use the election process to place weak administrative judges in office, the advantages of election by other judges nevertheless offset any potential disadvantages.

Removing judicial executives from the fragmenting effects of local political influences is the most immediate requirement for effective judicial leadership. Chief judges who are required to accomplish court objectives through political compromise and bargaining cannot be expected to be effective managers. Compromise and informal negotiations take precedence over the requirements of efficient administration. According to the proponents of merit selection, the present system of electing judges exposes them to a number of deleterious influences. Vigorous administration by elected judges during tenure as chief judge may make them unpopular with local entities that often exercise influence with the voters. Under these conditions, as chief judges, they would conform to the hypothesis that officials in highly discretionary jobs exercise their powers "whenever they believe it is to their advantage to do so and evade discretion on other occasions."[26] Elected administrators often discover that their continued presence in office is contingent upon the avoidance of any discretionary activity that causes undue displeasure or "publicity." Consequently, most reform groups say that the very least that must be done to protect judges from the wrath of local constituencies is to protect them from "ballot-box retaliation."[27] Almost every reform program of the last twenty years has advocated merit selection of judges. Approximately twenty-five states presently use some form of merit appointment.

Since a vast majority of circuit judges in Florida are appointed to the bench as replacements for judges who die or retire, the elective nature of their office is not as significant as it might be. Also, few judges are ever turned out of office by the voters.[28] As is also important to note, little empirical evidence has been generated to support the contention that elected judges are inferior to appointed judges in any aspect of their performance.[29] Thus, suggesting that merit appointment is a panacea would be foolhardy.

Despite this caveat, merit appointment appears to be a logical component of the reform movement. A 1976 Florida constitutional amendment implemented merit selection of appellate court judges. The fact that including circuit and county judges in this plan was "politically impossible"[30] is significant. Apparently the judges' ties to their local constituencies are sentimental, if not actual, factors that may negatively influence their administrative behavior.

Although the rationale for the adoption of such a selection technique is seldom related to administration, existence of such an appointment mechanism in Florida may potentially exert advantageous effects on chief judges' management capabilities. In addition to partially removing administration from "politics," merit selection screens potential candidates on the basis of their qualifications and would provide the opportunity to implement a simplified mechanism by which incompetent and/or corrupt judges can be removed from office. Thus, the general quality of the judiciary is potentially upgraded. The selection system that has attracted the most attention is termed the "Missouri Plan." The components of this selection technique are roughly as follows: (1) formation of a panel of judicial candidates by a nonpartisan commission composed of qualified lawyers and laymen; (2) appointment by the governor of judges from the candidates provided by the commission (usually three candidates are provided for each vacancy); and (3) review of the appointment by the voters after a short probationary term of service. The judge runs unopposed "on his record" and must obtain a majority of votes to be retained in office. Under the previously mentioned 1976 constitutional amendment, appellate court judges are appointed by a mechanism that closely resembles this plan.

The final variable that potentially affects the chief judges' ability to properly manage their circuits is unaffected by the degree of expertise and political neutrality present among judicial administrators. Specifically, the level of interference from other court managers and political entities is of fundamental importance. Reform in this area cannot be accomplished until the courts are freed from their dependence upon local political systems, a goal that is predicated upon an altered conception of the court clerks' role.

Court Clerks

Effective utilization of administrative authority by chief judges cannot be achieved until the court clerks' role in the judicial structure is radically altered. The grave lack of administrative direction present within the court system may be largely attributed to the influence of court clerks. Because they control such a large proportion of the court's support functions and operating revenues, court clerks occupy a strategic power position from which judicial commands can be effectively resisted. Moreover, the elective nature of their office furnishes the clerks with a localistic orientation that often proves to be counterproductive to judicial efficiency. Bureaucratic organizations cannot function adequately when many of their most responsible members are independently elected officials whose primary allegiance is to their electorate. Consistent and uniform administration thus cannot be realized until court clerks become responsive to judicial authority. The achievement of this goal is predicated on two major reforms: (1) split each court clerk's office pursuant to Article V, Section 16 of the Florida Constitution; and (2) eliminate the present system of selecting clerks by popular election.

Splitting the Office. Court clerks have traditionally been granted a variety of duties that encompass two branches of government, executive and judicial.[31] As county recorder, county finance officer, county comptroller, county auditor, county treasurer, and secretary/accountant for the county commission, court clerks perform functions that clearly involve executive responsibility, and the number of their judicial duties has been increasing since the implementation of Article V. The overlap of functions places clerks in the tenuous position of serving two masters and results in conflicting allegiances between state and local objectives, policy priorities, and accountability requirements.

Distributing the present duties of court clerks between two offices, one judicial and one executive, is an essential prerequisite to granting the judiciary the independent administrative posture to which it is constitutionally entitled. The benefits to be gained through such a distribution of responsibilities are apparent. Primarily, the court clerks' responsiveness to judicial authority should increase. By severing their county-based duties from the judicial structure, clerks will be less inclined to adhere to extremely localistic policy preferences. Their loyalty will no longer be divided between the goals of county commissioners and courts. Consequently, judicial objectives may be internalized and role conflict may decline. Moreover, the chief judges' constitutional role as chief administrative officer should assume added significance when court clerks no longer regard county commissioners as their "bosses" or colleagues. The clerks' accountability and responsiveness to judicial authority should thus be enhanced.

In addition to the rather abstract advantages of accountability and responsiveness, separating the clerks' executive and judicial functions would lead to the establishment of a full-time administrative role for the clerks and should result in more competent court management. Court clerks who perform only purely judicial functions will logically devote a much larger percentage of their time to "court work" than is presently the case. As a consequence, clerks may be expected to abandon their former crisis management philosophy for a more active administrative role within the judicial system. Among the major benefits that should result are: long-range planning designed to isolate and resolve administrative problems before they become serious detriments to the organization; the development of managerial expertise among the clerks; and more concerted attempts to eradicate the redundant and inefficient forms and procedures that are now so prevalent. Indeed, full-time administrative direction by court clerks will quite probably eliminate much of the present management vacuum and thus should facilitate implementation of reform policies.

Selection of Clerks. Separation of the court clerks' offices is thus the most expedient and feasible method of establishing judicial authority. A further measure that is advisable, yet presently politically infeasible, is to eliminate popular elections of clerks. In all but a few states and several local jurisdictions, popular elections are used to select these officers.[32] As has been previously noted, the independent status that election gives to clerks has, in Florida as well as many other states, facilitated resistance to judicial authority.

Whether or not the judiciary would ever be able to control court clerks as long as they are elected is highly questionable. Although creation of a clerk's position that encompasses only judicial functions will clarify the roles of court managers, responsiveness to the judiciary cannot be assured until the court clerks' responsibility to their constituencies is nullified. Elected officials do not readily perceive themselves as bureaucrats in an organizational hierarchy who must obey the orders of their superiors. The authority of presiding judges is insufficient to insure cooperation from elected clerks who often utilize their elected status to legitimize defiant behavior. Centralization of administrative authority in the chief judges' offices is thus an idle fantasy while court clerks retain their independent status. The dilemma of a chief judge attempting to administer a court system where elected officials abound has been described thusly: "His duties are like those of the impressario of a ballet in which the ballet dancers are not hired by him, or paid by him or fired by him, but he is expected to make them dance with grace, beauty, and charm."[33]

Political selection of court clerks is detrimental not only to judicial authority, but to court efficiency. Court clerks in Florida are apparently seldom selected on the basis of managerial expertise. Rather, the elective method of selection has resulted in a group of court managers who are often without training or experience in court procedures and/or administration. Parochialism predominates over a realistic concern for efficiency. Moreover, the expenses of running for office, and the time expended in reelection efforts, indubitably detracts from the clerks' effectiveness and potentially exposes the judicial system to charges of impropriety.[34]

Popular election of court clerks is a carryover from Jacksonian Democracy that is both dysfunctional and illogical. Court clerks are not policymakers in the true meaning of the term. The public is ignorant of what the clerk does and how he does it. Moreover, the public has no viable means by which to evaluate the performance of such officers. Consequently, the electorate cannot properly judge whether or not any particular clerk is accomplishing his objectives efficiently.[35] Thus, elections for clerks resemble the proverbial "popularity contests" between local "politicos" in which incumbents rarely lose.

"Improvements in the judicial system cannot be achieved without the participation and cooperation of the clerks' offices. If the judiciary is to improve itself, it must have control over those functions that directly serve it."[36] Therefore, the *ideal* solution would be to allow chief judges to appoint court clerks either by county or circuit. Although there are a number of arguments in favor of granting the appointing power to the state supreme court,[37] appointment by circuit judges is a more viable alternative. Specifically, court clerks should be appointed by the persons to whom they will ultimately be responsible. This selection technique would partially insure that the candidate for the clerk's office is "accepted" by the judges. Moreover, appointment by circuit judges would be more "palatable" to the counties that naturally object to the increased trend toward state controls and centralization. A person appointed by circuit judges is likely to be more cognizant of local political and judicial exigencies than would the person selected by a centralized authority.

Despite the obvious advantages of appointing court clerks, this selection technique does not guarantee that competent persons will be employed. In order to avoid political favoritism and/or "cronyism" some type of formalized selection procedure should be instituted. Such procedures should at least include: minimum standards that each candidate must fulfill before he is considered for the position; a judicial committee to recruit qualified candidates; and a mechanism by which the applicants are reviewed and selected solely on the basis of their qualifications. The judicial system would accrue great benefits by implementing routinized personnel procedures. Besides improving the quality and level of professionalism among court clerks, the judges' power of appointment and removal is an expedient technique to insure the clerks' loyalty and responsiveness to judicial goals.

Court Executive Assistants

The current status of court executive assistants in Florida is extremely precarious. Largely as a result of the negative and/or apathetic attitudes of court clerks and judges, professional court administrators have been granted very few significant management responsibilities. Most of the underlying reasons why the position has not enjoyed much success will be effectively negated if chief judges assume administrative control over the circuits. Because many chief judges have not internalized the constitutional depiction of their office as the center of administrative authority, only trivial duties remain to be delegated to court executives. This situation will be radically altered when chief judges begin to exercise control over all phases of court administration. The realities of administering a complex organization may compel the judges to seek assistance from the court executives, regardless of judicial desires to the contrary.[38] As administrative responsibilities consume increasing proportions of the judges' energies, archaic biases against "administration" quite probably will be replaced by at least a tacit acceptance of professional managers. The tendency of chief judges to utilize their court executives may also be affected positively by the improved "quality" of the judiciary, which is a potential byproduct of nonpolitical selection and increased training. Chief judges presently administer through elaborate political compromises that are jeopardized by "expertise." However, the necessity for expertise and competent administration should become apparent to a judiciary that has been trained in management procedures and that no longer depends upon political factors to provide cooperation and support from local governmental entities.

Alteration of the role of court clerks will also exert a significant impact upon the acceptance of court executive assistants as well as upon the nature of their duties. By removing the court clerks' policy-making influence and making them responsible to judicial authority, much of the present political and individual opposition to court executives will dissipate. Court clerks will no longer occupy a power position from which they are able to aggressively resist encroachment by professional administrators, and the clerks' role perceptions should not be seriously threatened by officials whose organizational status and functions correspond rather closely to their own. Without substantive policy-making control over personnel and budgets, the court clerks' position will indubitably resemble that of the court executive assistants. Professional administrators could thus be expected to occupy a much more meaningful position in the judicial bureaucracy than is presently possible.

Creating Two Specialties. The fact that the roles, functions, and duties of court clerks and court executive assistants would almost completely converge if the reforms proposed for the clerks' office were instituted suggests an interesting contradiction. Since both groups of managers would receive instructions from the chief judges and would therefore share in the supervision of all judicial and quasi-judicial support functions, one position should obviously be abolished or a realistic separation of responsibilities be contrived. Employing two distinct groups of administrators to perform identical functions would clearly be absurd. In smaller circuits obviously court administrators cannot easily be justified. In fact, their presence represents a distinct waste of judicial resources. However, urbanized circuits may often require the services of as many trained administrators as they are able to obtain. The most practical technique that may be utilized to overcome the apparent redundancy of personnel is to separate judicial from nonjudicial administrative duties. By specifically differentiating the duties that are basically judicial from those that involve general management functions, two distinct specialties will be developed within the field of court administration.[39]

The responsibilities of the first group of specialists would closely resemble the duties now supposedly performed by court executive assistants. Personnel specializing in this area of court administration might justifiably be referred to as "judges' assistants." Their primary functions would be to assume partial responsibility over various judicial functions that ordinarily are the province of chief judges. Among the duties that judges' assistants should take part in are: calendar and docket management, budget preparation and control, jury system management, correspondence, statistical compilation and analysis, liaison with other government agencies, and secretarial support to administrative meetings of the judges.[40]

The major rationale for employing specialized personnel to perform these functions is to relieve chief judges of as many administrative duties as possible. The assumption of such management tasks by trained assistants would not only make the position of chief judge more attractive, but would also grant the judges additional time to pursue more immediate policy objectives. The performance of such duties presupposes a sizable degree of expertise in judicial affairs. Consequently, prospective judges' assistants must possess a measure of training and experience in some court-related profession.

The second group of specialists would replace court clerks. These personnel would supervise the "general administrative" aspects of judicial organizations. Although court clerks have traditionally controlled such facets of the court system, the "new breed" administrators would not possess budgetary and personnel control and thus would be unable to manage their support functions in a manner contradictory to the wishes of chief judges. The general administrative duties to be performed by these managers include:

Organization and administration. Organize and supervise all of the nonjudicial activities of the courts, including clerical and processing functions.

Employee Supervision. Direct the work of all nonjudicial officers and employees of the courts. Manage the judicial personnel department.

Space and equipment management. Maintain inventory of court physical property and provide adequate equipment and supplies to court staff. Administer and schedule courtroom space in concert with the judges' assistant.

Clerical duties. Record and maintain all court documents and act as auditor and finance officer for monies collected by the court.

A number of benefits will result from this altered conception of the court clerks' role. By converting clerks into professionalized "management specialists," the nonjudicial facets of court administration should function more efficiently. As with the judges' assistants, these specialists will require extensive management expertise, and although their skills will be more "managerial" than judicial, the influx of competent and responsible administrators can be expected to eliminate a large number of judicial inefficiencies. Moreover, cooperation between the two groups of administrators may be facilitated by their "professionalization." (However, the presence of two specialties responsible to the same person might result in petty jealousies and friction as each group attempts to secure the favor of judges.) This phenomenon, in turn, will aid in the coordination of the various activities that characterize all judicial organizations.

Institutionalization of these two specialties within the field of court management is contingent upon judicial appointment of the court clerks or management specialists. As has been stated, such a reform is hardly likely in most states, and especially in Florida. Thus, the feasibility of the plan is extremely questionable. However, elimination of popular election of court clerks has been a major component of many recent reform proposals. The rapid progress of other phases of court reform prove that almost anything is possible in this field. If judicial appointment of clerks does become a reality, the roles of court administrators relative to these personnel will have to be clarified.

It is also true that court clerks may be effective judicial administrators *despite* their elected status. The splitting of the clerks' county and judicial functions is of primary importance. After this reform, continued election of clerks in most states might serve "as a positive counterbalance in encouraging local identification and initiative which, if channeled properly, would result in a more dynamic and responsive system as a whole."[41] Thus, incremental steps toward ultimate "unification" may suffice or indeed by superior to a complete establishment of a separate and independent judiciary.

An Alternative. Because of the fact that court clerks will continue to be elected for some time to come in Florida, the Staff of the Joint Select Committee on Judicial Personnel of the Florida Legislature has suggested an alternative to the present organizational design of the Florida court system. The proposal was developed in order to address the problem of providing chief judges with sufficient administrative support to supervise and coordinate their court systems.

Instead of employing sixty-seven court clerks to supervise the nonjudicial functions of the courts situated in their counties, the staff states that utilizing only twenty would be desirable. Specifically, a chief circuit clerk (a more appropriate title might be "chief circuit administrator") would be elected in each circuit to oversee all the clerks' duties within his jurisdiction. This official would be directly responsible to the chief judge and would possess no independent authority. The chief circuit clerk would appoint a deputy administrator in each county of the circuit or in branch offices of single-county circuits. Deputy administrators would replace court clerks and would be responsible to the chief circuit clerk directly and to the chief judge ultimately.[42]

This proposal would parallel the judicial organization of the chief judge— court executive assistant relationship and offers several advantages over the court clerk system. Because there would only be twenty chief circuit clerks, chief judges would only be compelled to directly supervise one official involved with quasi-judicial functions. That official, in turn, would be responsible for the actions of the deputy administrators he appoints to manage the courts in the other counties in the circuit. Consequently, chief judges would be freed from the necessity of continually supervising and delegating authority to large numbers of subordinates. This would simplify communication and administrative direction within the circuits. The chief circuit clerks would possess fewer responsibilities than chief judges and would thus have adequate time to evaluate the performance of deputy administrators. Finally, a step toward the *regionalization* of court administration would be taken. A regional, as opposed to county, response to court management is an exciting alternative that is becoming increasingly popular. Samuel D. Conti, in recommending a regional approach to court unification in Massachusetts, is one of a growing number of proponents of this reform style. According to Conti, "regionalism permits both efficient administration in an area and responsiveness to local needs and demands which are likely to vary throughout the state."[43]

This is clearly a more palatable dish to local governments than is total unification and centralization. Such an organizational form might become "the answer" to the search for an alternative to our presently accepted panaceas for court fragmentation. Numerous states, including New York, California, and Michigan, are considering systems of regional administration as opposed to more localized administrative structures."[44] However, instead of allowing for local selection of regional administrators and presiding judges, these plans frequently call for centralized appointment. Such selection techniques may obviate the potential advantages foreseen by proponents of regionalization. Because the powers of appointment and control are often synonymous, regional presiding judges and court administrators who owe their offices to the central authority may be disinclined to value regional prerogatives over state dictates. Thus, local appointment of regional administrators is presently the only feasible selection technique available in Florida.

Systemic Reforms

Redefinition of the court managers' roles is a necessity if Florida's judicial system is to be reformed effectively. When administrative supremacy is success-fully granted to the judiciary, the negative effects of fragmentation, localism, and nonprofessionalism should dwindle. However, two major reforms must be instituted before alterations in the court managers' roles can be ultimately achieved. The state government must assume some responsibility for the courts' budget and personnel systems. It is entirely illogical to contemplate the judges' assumption of administrative direction when they do not command these two essential elements of their organization.

State Funding

The maleficent consequences of locally controlled court budgets appear through-out the present study. Disparate levels of court financing, inadequate application of technological innovation, and inconsistent procedures are a few of the management dilemmas that may be directly or indirectly attributed to the counties' role in judicial fiscal affairs. Perhaps an even more serious result is that court clerks, by virtue of their influence on the courts' budgets, possess a sizable degree of policy-making influence within the judicial system.

In consolidating Florida's court system the state government assumed "full responsibility for the fair, consistent, and effective administration of justice."[45] Yet, at least in Florida, accomplishment of this goal is not feasible if the state relies heavily on local funding.[46] State court financing is a crucial component of court administration, and few authorities deny that the judicial branch should ultimately control its own monetary resources. The financing of trial courts by local governments tends to obscure the lines of administrative authority that are ostensibly delimited by Article V. If the state government assumes the fiscal burden for all phases of explicitly judicial activity, authority and responsibility for court administration will be more firmly established in the judiciary and implementation of the reform programs should be promoted.

State assumption of judicial expenses has long been advocated by authori-ties on court administration. With few exceptions, centralized funding is regarded as the first major condition that must be fulfilled before true judicial reform can occur. In addition to removing the fragmenting effects of local politics from the judicial system, the following advantages of state funding have been cited by a variety of authors: (1) improved planning potential, (2) more equitable distribution of resources, (3) greater economy, (4) the ability to meet unusual contingencies, (5) greater efficiency, and (6) improved management information system.[47]

Traditional budgetary methods limit the ability of courts to plan. Accurate statements of the system's current expenditures, available resources, and expected needs are required in order to design strategy to confront future needs effectively. However, local budgeting and accounting techniques vary to such an extent that deriving valid conclusions from the information provided by counties is extremely difficult. Moreover, any reform that is implemented is certain to require the cooperation of counties with disparate abilities (and desires) to conform to state requests. Under these conditions, the implementation of true unification is largely a matter of "optimistic exhortation."[48]

Centralized budgeting mechanisms will eliminate these problems and thus enable the court system to plan for change constructively. More precise statements of judicial expenditures and available resources will inevitably result from standardized budgeting and accounting procedures. In addition, the court system will no longer be compelled to rely upon local politicians to finance and implement reform policies. By granting the supreme court the authority and resources necessary to execute state-wide policy options, planning could conceivably become a continuous and effective activity.

Due to unequal abilities of local governments to properly finance court administration, citizens in many counties do not receive the degree and quality of judicial services that are available to residents of more wealthy areas. The effectiveness of many courts is hampered by a lack of modern equipment and facilities that stems (both directly and indirectly) from inadequate tax bases. Reliance upon local funding requires some counties to pay "disproportionately high shares of the total cost of the court system."[49] For example, the presence of a penal institution, diversion center, and the like in a jurisdiction may create an abnormally large volume of writs for the courts in that area to review.[50]

Such inequities would clearly be remedied by a central budgeting authority that would be capable of comparing local court requirements and thereby distribute resources according to need. Courts presently functioning without modern clerical equipment and/or services would benefit from the resulting redistribution of resources. Judicial efficiency might thus be improved, and the quality of justice received by each citizen would no longer depend upon a person's county of residence.

Local funding contributes to a phenomenon that appears in most decentralized bureaucracies: overlapping and duplication of services, facilities, and equipment. For example, two of the more populous circuits within the state are directly adjacent to each other, yet both invested in separate and expensive computer systems. If these circuits had properly planned and coordinated their activities, they undoubtedly could have saved large sums of money by sharing one centrally located computer facility.

State funding would allow courts to avoid such wasteful and costly mistakes. In concert with planning activities, the supreme court could establish an internal department to supervise the coordination of purchasing activities. This procedure would also permit economy of scale. The acquisition of legal documents, furniture, and equipment in bulk would reduce costs and would also enable the courts to obtain consistent quality in the materials purchased. Moreover, automation of records-keeping and/or microfilm facilities on a centralized basis would be more economical than allowing each court to independently plan, develop, and finance its own such management aides.[51]

In the past decade courts in many cities and states have been unexpectedly confronted by enormous numbers of arrests that they were ill-equipped to process. For example, according to the National Advisory Commission on Civil Disorders, riots in eight cities during 1967 resulted in so many arrests that local trial courts were "immobilized."[52] Although Florida has yet to experience such an occurrence, the prospects that one will occur cannot be discounted. Under the present financing system, whether any county in the state could adequately cope with such an emergency is extremely doubtful. A unified budgeting mechanism would provide both immediate financial assistance and a simplified method of reassiging personnel and equipment to the area.[53]

Local funding has been cited as an important contributory cause of many current judicial inefficiencies. Form and procedural redundancies and inequities are largely the result of local politicians who perceive their budgetary control as justification for implementing whatever operational techniques they desire. Reform in these areas of court administration has been quite difficult to accomplish because without control over their own budgets, chief judges do not collectively possess enough political power to force court clerks to implement more consistent practices.

State funding would also enable state judicial officials to implement a mechanism to inspect and evaluate all forms and procedures currently in use. Such a review program would hopefully isolate the most inefficient organizational processes and would therefore accelerate the design and implementation of superior judicial practices. State funding also would enable judicial authorities to compare costs between and among different courts and jurisdictions. Such information would be useful in transferring judges, ordering equipment, planning for new judicial departments and judges, and the like. Finally, criteria could be established to assist in evaluating budget requests and expenditures.[54]

The present case disposition reporting system has several flaws. Many chief judges do not believe that the statistics produced by the system are accurate. Several counties are reluctant to submit case disposition reports, and procedural variations in the other counties serve to decrease the validity of the statistics that are reported. For example, responsibility for calendar management and case tracking is given to clerks in some instances and to states attorneys or court administrators on other occasions, which has resulted in irregular reporting techniques as well as in varying interpretations of legal actions. In other counties the number of dispositions is often inflated by the clerks' tendency to report each offense of a person arrested for multiple charges as an individual "case."[55] Finally, there are few provisions for "case weighting"—that is, a complicated and exhaustive labor relations suit is assigned no more "weight" than is a simple civil case consuming fifteen minutes of the judge's time. This fact has created concern among judges who hear time-consuming cases.

State funding of the entire judicial system is perceived as being a partial solution to these statistical difficulties. The movement toward uniform procedures that will be precipitated by state funding may also lead to standardization of report and classification procedures. The state government could thus benefit not only from an improved CDR system, but from information gathered on other aspects of court administration. If such factors as courtroom capacities, records volume, and exhibit storage space were added to the computer capability that has already been developed for the CDR system, the judicial system would have a much greater capacity to plan for the courts' future building requirements.

Implementation of State Funding. State funding will not magically result in an efficient and economical judicial system that is capable of planning for its own needs. State funding must be preceded or accompanied by several other innovations that will enable the judiciary to properly utilize its new powers and resources. The Florida judicial system has partially fulfilled these preconditions that were first outlined by Edward Pringle: (1) an administrative structure vesting ultimate budgetary responsibility in one office, (2) an administrative staff to assist in budgeting duties, and (3) a form of participatory management.[56]

Responsibility for the budget must be centrally located in one office—a situation that presupposes a uniform judicial structure. The reorganization accomplished by Article V established an administrative structure that lends itself admirably to a centrally controlled budget. Since the chief justice of the Florida Supreme Court is the constitutionally designated chief administrative officer of the judicial system, that person would logically assume ultimate responsibility for major budgetary activities. Moreover, the clearly established line of authority that descends from the chief justice's office to the chief judges could serve as a vehicle by which budget policy could be formulated and controlled.

The second aspect of judicial organization that must precede state funding is the presence of an agency or department that can assist the chief justice with his fiscal duties. According to the National Advisory Commission on Criminal Justice Standards and Goals, "A budget for the operation of the entire court system of the state should be prepared by the state court administrator and submitted to the appropriate legislative body."[57] Again, Florida already possesses such an office. The present Office of State Courts Administrator should function as the financial center for the courts. Budget preparation, administration, accounting, and auditing could best be performed by professional budget personnel who are employed by the courts. A recurring failure of court systems has been that they infrequently attempt to define their goals and objectives in terms of: "What are we trying to do, and how should we be trying to do it?"[58] By preparing and auditing the budget in a central office, answers to these questions should be stimulated and perfected. Such a technique would be invaluable in preparing responsible and legitimate appropriations requests.

The third aspect that should be present in the judicial system in order to assure that the unitary budget is properly administered is some form of participatory management.[59] Although judicial councils and advisory boards of judges would be functional in providing judicial input into the chief justice's budgetary policy decisions, the existence of twenty chief judges who are already directly responsible for regional policy dictates that no special judicial consultative body is required. Rather, chief judges must be given the opportunity to meet collectively in order to discuss mutual fiscal problems and to prepare programs and objectives for submission to the chief justice. "Judges conferences," which are scheduled periodically for these purposes, appear to be extremely promising in this regard.

In order to insure that no circuit is unfairly deprived of resources, establishing a formula to allocate funds according to legitimate criteria would also be advisable. This formula could possibly be calculated according to population, litigation rates, or prior expenditure levels. The actual figure that is "settled upon" should be open to alteration depending upon the justification each jurisdiction offers for extra funding. Such a mechanism would partially obviate the ultimate distortion of centralization—that is, demeaned judges begging for money and being deprived of needed resources on personalistic and/or arbitrary bases. As Carl Baar has advocated, formula grants could be utilized in implementing state financing. This technique has been successfully employed in Pennsylvania and reportedly preserves local judicial administrative autonomy and integrity while it allows the judiciary to eliminate many of the more tangible dilemmas of fragmented funding.[60] However, at least in Florida the negative consequences of present funding practices dictate caution. Unless court clerks are subjected to judicial authority, formula grants may well perpetuate the fragmented system that exists. Some measure of centralized judicial control must be instituted.

Any program of state funding must also be grounded on the precept that legislative and executive interference should be kept to a minimum. The traditional depiction of the courts as "state agencies" can be avoided most expeditiously by granting the judiciary a percentage of the state budget, exclusive of extensive pre- and postaudit controls. Although the exact percentage of the state budget that would be required to support the judicial branch is approximately 3 percent,[61] there is little likelihood that the Florida legislature will adopt such a plan. State governments throughout the nation have been extremely hesitant to implement similar funding techniques.

An Alternative: Inherent Powers. In the event that the state government rejects the burden of full state funding, the court system could conceivably invoke the inherent power doctrine.[62] Simply stated, this doctrine assumes that every court has an inherent power to do whatever is reasonably necessary to administer justice within its jurisdiction properly. In its most practical application, the doctrine implies that the courts can do anything necessary to maintain their existence and to permit their operation. If the courts decide that the legislature is hindering their ability to conduct business due to inadequate appropriations, they can assert their status as an independent branch of government by forcing the legislature to provide funds.[63] Despite the apparent attractiveness of this legal remedy for the courts' financial ills, there are few precedents in which a judicial branch has initiated such action against a state legislature. This fact is hardly surprising considering the political ramifications that would inevitably result from a blatant confrontation between the judicial and legislative branches of government.

Although the courts are extremely reluctant to challenge state legislatures, the doctrine of inherent powers has been invoked on numerous occasions in regard to local funding sources. In almost every state[64] cases have arisen in which courts sued county governments for a variety of goods and services ranging from judicial salaries[65] to acoustics.[66] Among the other areas in which the doctrine has been utilized most effectively are: determining the necessity for employees;[67] requiring payments to support personnel;[68] and providing adequate space for judicial functions.[69] The judiciary in the states where these cases were decided have apparently adopted an interpretation of the inherent and separation of powers doctrines espoused by Jim R. Carrigan. He states that courts have an "affirmative obligation to assert and fully exercise" their powers in an attempt to remain independent and to operate efficiently.[70]

The inherent powers doctrine has seldom appeared in Florida case law. The most articulate definition of the doctrine that has emanated from the Florida Supreme Court appeared in a 1952 action. In that year the Florida Bar Association requested the court to take charge of money paid to the Board of Law Examiners and to employ an administrative officer. The association contended that such action could be taken both under a 1951 statute that empowered the court to prescribe additional duties, powers, and procedures for the board and under the inherent powers of the court.[71]

The court denied the request by stating that the statute in question pertained only to the qualifications of examinees for admission to the bar and that the doctrine of separation of powers was such that only the legislature could create officers or positions.[72] The court's comments regarding inherent powers are particularly noteworthy:

It is true that courts of general jurisdiction have certain inherent or implied powers that stem from the constitutional or statutory provisions creating the court and clothing it with jurisdiction. In other words, regularly constituted courts have power to do anything that is reasonably necessary to administer justice within the scope of its jurisdiction, but not otherwise. Inherent powers has to do with the incidents of litigation, control of the conduct of its officers and the preservation of order and decorum with reference to its proceedings. Such is the scope of inherent power, unless the authority of the court clothes it with more. The legislature has not seen fit to enlarge the inherent power of this court, so we are without power to authorize the appointment of an administrative officer of the State Board of Law Examiners.[73]

Thus, the inherent power doctrine in Florida is defined rather narrowly as "merely an extension of jurisdictional power."[74] The employment of officers and the expenditure of public funds to pay their salaries are viewed as legislative prerogatives over which the judiciary has no power, unless through specific legislative authorization. While this general interpretation may have been modified slightly by a 1968 case,[75] its use is extremely rare. Although judicial activists may view the phenomenon negatively, two major arguments against the utilization of inherent powers indicate that Florida's application of the doctrine may indeed be wise.

According to Geoffrey Hazard, Martin McNamera, and Irwin Sentilles, as the doctrine is applied in cases throughout the nation, it is usually narrowly defined and thus involves only "marginal appropriations for ancillary personnel and facilities rather than basic fiscal underwriting."[76] Therefore, the definition and interpretation of the doctrine would have to be greatly expanded before it could provide a steady source of revenue. Most courts involved in this form of legal action have justified invoking inherent powers on the basis of guaranteeing that "indispensable" items are provided by local governments. This issue of "indispensability" invites county commissions to analyze all judicial expenditures, and one view has been that the only truly indispensible aspect of the judicial budget is the judges' salaries.[77] Moreover, reliance upon inherent powers is potentially detrimental to efficiency. Legally compelling local governments to finance court administration leaves no opportunity to evaluate rationally the wisdom of budget choices. Thus, traditional practices are retained.[78] As a result of these factors, the most realistic and utilitarian approach to court financing appears to be state assumption of all judicial expenditures.

State Personnel Control

Reform groups commonly complain that the judicial system is unique among all governmental branches and agencies in that it must rely upon other entities for its personnel. This phenomenon has resulted in management dilemmas, including incompetent and poorly trained employees. Moreover, local control over judicial personnel is one of the numerous factors that contributes to the chief judges' inability and/or reluctance to manage. The judiciary cannot be held fully responsible for its own operations unless it has control over its own employees.[79] A viable alternative to local control of this aspect of court administration is for the state government to implement a judicial personnel system. The creation of a separate personnel system is imperative if the judiciary is to maintain itself as an independent branch of government. To do otherwise would perpetuate the present system that exposes the judiciary to the vagaries of local politics, patronage, and administrative incompetence.

With two major exceptions, all quasi-judicial personnel within the Florida court system should be selected, supervised, and promoted in accordance with regulations adopted by the supreme court.[80] The judges' personal staff, including legal clerks and secretaries, should be exempted in order to provide the judges with control over their confidential employees. All other full-time county personnel who exclusively serve the court system should become state employees. However, exempting maintenance, security, and police agency personnel as well, as was done in Alabama in 1977,[81] would also be advisable. Each person employed by the courts should be directly responsible to the judiciary and should meet standard selection and performance criteria. A uniform personnel policy should include the following elements: uniform classification, compensation, and recruitment procedures; merit incentives and promotion programs; standardized benefit and vacation provisions; uniform retirement and termination procedures; and effective obligatory training programs. The Staff of the Joint Select Committee on Judicial Personnel of the Florida legislature has already prepared the essential elements of this personnel system. They lobbied unsuccessfully for its adoption in both 1974 and 1975. Although the Florida legislature continues to "consider" the program, its chances of passage are currently minute due to local resistance and the fear that the expense would be prohibitive.

In order to placate proponents of local personnel control, implementing a personnel system that allows for both state and local participation is advisable. An administrative appendage to the Florida Supreme Court should be established to develop uniform procedures, salary scales, job classifications, and other conditions of employment. Personnel managers located within the circuit administrators' offices could then allow for local participation and flexibility by performing all functions related to personnel management in the region. Through this division of responsibility the chief judges will be granted a degree of control over personnel administration, yet the most fundamental aspects of uniformity would be protected. In addition, the transitional stage in a decentralized administrative approach would be less disruptive, the personnel staff required at the state level would be kept to a minimum, and salaries and classifications could be tailored to the local "marketplace."[82]

The staff recommended in 1974 that court clerks be granted responsibility for administering the personnel system in the counties.[83] This proposal is illogical without radically altering the clerks' present role. If court clerks are not made responsive to chief judges, accountability to the central personnel system would be impossible to achieve. Another result would be a distortion of federalism by allowing county officers to control and administer state and regional policies. On the other hand, if court clerks are transformed into "nonjudicial specialists," then vesting personnel responsibilities in their offices would be the most expedient method of implementing the personnel system.

Establishment of centralized and standardized personnel procedures represents a major step toward improving the quality of quasi-judicial personnel. The judiciary is best able to train, evaluate, and administer the personnel it employs. It is also more qualified to determine qualifications and divisions of responsibility for its employees than are local officials whose court experience is minimal.

A unified personnel system facilitates recruitment and retention of qualified employees. The establishment of uniform salary structures, fringe benefits, and promotion criteria will make judicial system positions more attractive and lucrative to competent applicants. Employees who are performing identical functions in different courts will receive similar compensation and thus will be less likely to resign in order to accept higher paying jobs in other counties. Uniformity throughout the regions provides the opportunity for intercourt transfer to ease the workload and provides opportunities for employees to move without loss of position or benefits.[84] Standardization of vacation time, fringe benefits, and sick leave will eliminate current disparities that destroy employee morale by making many persons feel as if they are being unjustly treated.[85]

In addition to upgrading the quality of court employees, a uniform personnel system should also improve judicial efficiency. Development and implementation of uniform administrative forms and procedures will be facilitated by a corps of proficient employees whose allegiance to the courts is unquestioned. Moreover, in the course of pre-entry training, candidates for quasi-judicial positions may be instructed in the use of modern management procedures designed by the court managers. Through this technique, many of the obsolete and inefficient practices that have traditionally permeated the courts may be eliminated. Finally, by clearly delineating each employee's responsibilities, salary, and performance expectations, the courts' ability to establish and achieve specific management goals will be enhanced. Because employees' performance will not be rewarded except in terms of their responses to the duties they are assigned, efficiency should become an incentive for all personnel.

Summary

A fundamental prerequisite to effective court reform is establishment of the judiciary as an equal and independent branch of government. This goal can only be achieved if judges are granted the powers and resources necessary to administer and coordinate their organizations. Among the most urgent conditions that must be present in order to accomplish these complementary goals are: an altered conception of court clerks that enables the courts to control their support functions, administrative awareness and ability among judges, and competent administrative assistants to reduce the management burdens of judges. State assumption of judicial expenses, including personnel, offers the most immediate and pragmatic solution. By reducing fragmentation and diffused management authority, judges will conceivably assume their legitimate position as the formulators and implementers of reform policies.

Despite the apparent merits of the reforms outlined in the present chapter, a large number of political and cognitive factors may prove to be insurmountable obstacles to their acceptance. Court reform may be typified as a battle against tradition.[86] Court clerks, judges, and other personnel and aspects of the judicial system are greatly influenced by traditional procedures, management practices, and distributions of responsibility. Chapter 5 examines these variables in light of their inhibiting effects on administrative and systemic judicial reform.

5 Obstacles to Reform

Wherever alterations of court organizations and procedures have been advocated, an amazing variety of social, political, and institutional influences have arisen to combat reformers. The resulting altercations between proponents of change and exponents of the status quo are useful in exemplifying the controversial nature of court reform. Between 1961 and 1971, a majority of all court modernization proposals were defeated by state legislatures, constitutional revision commissions, or voters.[1] Thus, in 1966, the California legislature rejected a bill that would have consolidated the state's trial courts in a battle that is still raging; in 1967, legislation designed to consolidate and unify the Rhode Island courts was allowed to die in committee; in 1970, new constitutions containing unified judicial articles were rejected by the voters in Idaho and Arkansas; also in 1970, the Iowa legislature defeated a proposed amendment to reorganize the lower court structure;[2] and in 1973, the Nevada legislature not only refused to implement unitary funding, but also abolished the position of state court administrator.

Despite these defeats, the pace of reform has accelerated. The pages of *Judicature* and the *State Court Journal* are brimming with reports of successful reform movements in almost every state. However, the process of change continues to be erratic. The forces of tradition only grudgingly yield to modernization. While the superficial components of reform, such as consolidation, the adoption of merit selection, and elimination of nonattorney judges, frequently appear, the substantive impact of such "improvements" is an unknown quantum. Once reforms are implemented, countervailing forces serve to divest many reforms of their intended effects.

The present chapter examines the primary obstacles to achievement of viable judicial reform in Florida. The dubious success of Article V has already been chronicled, and as is apparent, traditionalism and vested interests have primarily been culpable for the deficient state of reform induced by Article V. In addition, there are a number of related factors that are endemic to court organizations and may prevent adoption of the reforms discussed in the preceding chapter. These include: the impact of legal culture, the attitudes of court managers, and consequences of the macro-political environment.

The Legal Culture

The legal system is one of the most traditional and "sacrosanct"[3] governmental institutions. The United States is known as a nation of "Constitution worshippers." Another cliché that enjoys wide currency is that this is a county of laws, not men. Thus, jurisprudence is an object of respect and reverence. This distinctive status of law in America is fundamental to an understanding of court reform specifically and court administration generally. Of particular importance are: the legal tradition from which American law developed, peculiar characteristics of the administration of justice that constrain management, and the anti-administrative nature of American jurisprudence.

Although scholars have advanced a number of explanations for the revered nature of American law, the most widely quoted theory postulates that this phenomenon stems from Western legal tradition.[4] Many of our "modern" legal precepts had their roots in canon law and in the Divine Right of early monarchs. Despite later secularization of law, numerous facets of American jurisprudence have retained a "quasi-sacred" character.[5]

Contemporary American law is greatly influenced by its relationship to the "sacred" practices of the past. Respect for the legal system is one of the most fundamental mores of American society. As explained by Herbert Jacob:

People are taught to respect law alone among the institutions of government, simply because it is law. Respect for the law is urged by many people as a necessary barrier to anarchy; they urge respect for the law even if one disagrees with it and seeks to change it.[6]

As a consequence of its unique status as a sacred and respected concept, law in the United States has been imbued with a degree of dignity and ceremony that is unprecedented in other government institutions. Unfortunately, court proceedings have also been saturated by a similar amount of ritualism. Manifestations of this phenomenon are rampant in any American courtroom. In the words of Alfred C. Conard, "The thousand-year-old Catholic mass has been turned into English, but lawyers are still telling their rosaries with habeas corpus, ultra vires, and res gestae."[7] Antiquated and ritualistic language is only one example of the courts' concern for tradition and respect. There are many others. The design of courtrooms and the behavior of participants in the legal process serve to enhance the sacred character of the judicial system. This phenomenon is immediately apparent to any layman who strays into the "mysterious" halls of justice. Even modes of speech and dress are carefully contrived to mystify the unknowing and to awe the naive.[8] Although each aspect of this drama has its purpose, the ultimate effect is to perpetuate tradition and to make the practitioners of the legal profession defensive about their sacred preserve.

The legal tradition that has invested courts with sacred and respected qualities is also responsible for many procedural and conceptual judicial characteristics that are counterproductive to administrative efficiency. These antiquated (and perhaps obsolete) operational practices and customs have been retained mainly because they have been sanctified by tradition. Despite the exigencies of current litigation levels, that such inefficient procedures will yield to the forces of reform is extremely unlikely. Due to the resistance of "sacrosanct" institutions to innovation, reform programs will probably have to be designed in accordance with the more traditional aspects of legal culture. The most administratively impractical and/or harmful characteristics of American jurisprudence are the adversary system, the jury system, and the nature of the legal profession.[9]

The adversary process is considered the "proper" method for resolving disputes in courtrooms. Originating from ancient customs involving trial by battle and/or confrontation, adversary proceedings are characterized by "verbal jousting," confrontation, and elaborate rules of procedure to insure a "fair fight" between litigants.

Several serious consequences for the administration of justice are generated by the adversary system. If the dispute in question requires a jury trial, a large number of persons must be assembled in one place in order to dispense justice adequately. Attorneys, a judge, witnesses, clerks, bailiffs, court reporters, and litigants are all required to be present.[10] In addition to the obvious logistic problems arising from this necessity, the expense incurred both by litigants and courts represents a serious malady. Moreover, the elaborate rules of evidence and procedure encourage attorneys to employ special tactics to gain an advantage for their clients. Legal maneuvers such as those arising from "surprise," "concealment," and continuances are often utilized to gain "tactical advantage."[11] These tactics often delay trials and thus greatly complicate the adjudicatory process.

The outcome of the adversary process also depends upon the competence of the attorneys and the complexity of the issues. Incompetent attorneys prevent fair presentations. Moreover, adversary hearings are inadequate forums to debate multifaceted issues that require specialized expertise, such as environmental and regulatory cases.[12]

A second vestige of ancient justice that inhibits court management is the jury system. Although the jury system is closely related to adversary proceedings, it is responsible for a unique set of constraints. Intricate and costly procedures are required to insure the selection of an adequate supply of impartial jurors. Often large urban courts are obliged to call thousands of persons for jury duty in order to fill one day's trial requirements. Courts encounter a major managerial problem in attempting to predict the number of necessary jurors. Establishing and operationalizing procedures to excuse persons from jury duty for hardship reasons and providing for juror's meals, transportation, and housing represent formidable management obstacles.[13] In addition, jury trials, like adversary proceedings, encourage legal maneuvering, exhaustive selection processes, and other "antics" that delay the judicial process.

Many scholars attribute much of the judicial system's "stand-pattism" to the nature of its personnel. Most of the people with policy-making and administrative authority in the courts are members of the legal profession.

Consequently, almost all significant judicial functions are directly controlled by attorneys. The fact that courts are primarily staffed by one profession gives them a cohesiveness that is not typical of other institutions. Unfortunately, the "cohesiveness" that attorneys display is frequently counterproductive to management. Because attorneys almost universally accept traditional judicial practices as being entirely legitimate and appropriate, change of any nature is viewed with suspicion.

Due to the fact that most court reforms include programs to routinize and standardize judicial behavior according to accepted management practices, innovation is now identified with administration. A large number of court management authorities contend that the judicial system refuses to reform itself simply because it does not desire to be "administered."[14] An anti-administration bias clearly exists among most members of the legal profession.[15] In fact, several authors have stated that the only time lawyers and judges become interested in administering the courts is during a crisis situation that disrupts judicial activity to the extent that public ire is aroused.

The legal profession's antipathy for administration can be traced to several sources. First, few attorneys have any administrative training or experience.[16] Until recently, law schools were extremely negligent in offering courses in management.[17] Moreover, attorneys and judges value their independence to such an extent that administration of any form is resisted. Administration presupposes that a degree of control will be exercised over members of an organization. Because control infringes upon their independence and threatens to transform them into mere "functionaries," attorneys and judges instinctively resist reforms that tend to bureaucratize the judicial system.[18] Finally, the courts' antipathy for administration may be traced to a philosophical conflict between justice and efficiency. "Due process is inefficient, deliberately so"[19] is a quote that capsulizes this controversy. Administration is viewed as being antithetical to fairness and to the adversary process. Speed and efficiency conflict with various procedural devices that attorneys rely upon to defend their clients. Although reformers contend that efficiency and justice are complementary goals, the legal community has been slow to appreciate the value of management.

The preceding discussion imparts a discouraging impression of the probability that comprehensive reforms will be implemented in judicial systems. American legal culture engenders numerous defenses against both change and administration. Moreover, the biases of judicial personnel toward innovation are reinforced by traditional practices and procedures that are revered by society but that restrain proper administration. Thus, the formidable and delicate task of reconciling the competing requirements of fairness and efficiency confronts reformers. The extent to which they are successful is partially dependent upon the strength of traditionalism among court managers.

Resistance from Court Managers

The reactions of chief judges and court clerks interviewed in this study to reforms intended by Article V suggest that further innovation within the Florida judicial system may be vigorously resisted. Logic dictates that any group of persons that has learned to work within a specific institutional arrangement will be reluctant to alter their behavior in order to adjust to a new system. The attitudes of court managers discussed in chapter 2 reflect the major obstacle to further reform. Because neither court clerks nor chief judges have internalized a "unified" depiction of Florida's court structure, these personnel can hardly be expected to countenance the comprehensive reforms outlined in the preceding chapter.

Under any judicial administrative system, chief judges must be the policy-makers for the courts. These court managers are therefore the key to any improvements in the administration of justice. Their willingness to accept a potent role in administration and their ability to perform their management functions effectively contribute to the eventual fate of court reform.[20] The "record" of lower court judges in reform movements has not been exceedingly encouraging to date. For example, superior court judges in California are faulted for resisting trial court consolidation in that state. Reforms in Alabama and Kentucky have also generated resistance on the part of lower trial court judges.[21]

Of critical importance in Florida are three major issues: (1) Do chief judges in Florida support a unified judicial system, including centralized budget and personnel procedures? (2) Will they voluntarily accept immense administrative responsibility? (3) Will court administrators be accepted as legitimate judicial management officers? Unless all three of these questions receive an affirmative response, the goal of a truly consolidated judicial system is probably unattainable.

The findings of this study show that most of the chief judges favor the court consolidation induced by Article V. However, the reasons for this favorable attitude are not necessarily an indication of the judiciary's support for complete unification. Interview responses indicate abolishment of specialized courts is viewed as a positive attribute because fragmentation has been reduced and the court system is thus considered to be more "streamlined," and Article V is seen as having reduced some of the worst abuses of locally controlled justice, such as political favoritism and corruption among judges in lower courts. While these attitudes imply that consolidation of judicial structure has been well-received, they do not indicate support for extensive centralization; rather, most chief judges appear to oppose further state control.

Only three judges specifically advocated state assumption of judicial budget or personnel responsibilities. They clearly assume that unitary financing will result in increased appropriations for their respective circuits. As one judge stated:

> State personnel and budget systems should help our present situation. We don't have adequate judges or staff to function adequately. State funding hopefully would create a uniformity in priorities where each circuit would be given enough personnel to at least clear its calendars. Some judges are sitting on their _____ while judges in other circuits work sixteen hours a day.

The remaining chief judges opposed centralized funding and personnel systems and justified their aversion with several arguments. A common complaint is that state government has never been responsive to the needs of the judiciary. Consequently, these judges fear that state fiscal controls will result in reduced appropriations. In addition, several judges objected to a perceived reduction of "local accountability," which, in turn, may influence voter response. Because they serve local constituencies, most chief judges apparently favor preservation of the fundamental budgetary link between the counties and the courts. Traditional political relationships between judges and court clerks are primarily based on county responsibility for judicial support functions, and since many circuits have experienced few problems in obtaining resources through political bargaining with the counties, chief judges are thus hesitant to "gamble" with an alternate system.

Another major obstacle to judicial acceptance of state budgetary and personnel controls is exemplified by the following exchange:

Interviewer: Do you favor state assumption of all judicial budget and personnel responsibilities?

Chief judge: Who would supervise the system if this were done?

Interviewer: The supreme court would ultimately be responsible, but the Office of State Courts Administrator would probably do most of the paper work.

Chief judge: You've got to be joking. _____ [state courts administrator] is building an empire in Tallahassee and now we're going to let him control our personnel and budgets? It'll never happen.

The chief judges' animosity for the state court administrator was obvious. Most chief judges clearly perceived the centralized administrative office as a threat to their independence and seemingly did not wish to cooperate with its representatives. This conviction was so marked that several judges apparently objected to any proposal that the state office advocated. For example, one judge, whose negative experiences with incompetent support personnel compelled him to become a proponent of state personnel controls, now opposes the system:

> As soon as _____ started screaming for "employee classification" and state pay for court personnel, I changed my mind. The administrator's office is very coy.

They say, "Look, judges, we want a judicial administrative set-up because secretaries and deputy clerks are classified under a botched-up system." What they don't say or tell to the legislature is that the judges don't support their pet scheme—they tell everybody the judges love it.

Whether chief judges objected to the state administrator personally, his office, or the reforms that his office represents is a moot point. Without cooperation between the circuits and the Office of State Courts Administrator, whether true uniformity can be achieved is doubtful. The central court administrative office must be a forceful advocate of uniform procedures and managerial standards or else it will be ineffectual. Judicial administrative officers who object to state controls or to the office formulating such controls are not likely to apply these directives conscientiously to their own circuits. In fact, some judges may avoid management responsibility in an attempt to undermine state judicial policy. Thus, the need for a gradual socialization of judges and for a gradual implementation of reform policies is called for. Radical changes will surely fail.

Every organization requires a responsible leader who is charged with the duty of ultimate supervision. Judges are the primary persons who are qualified to give such direction to court organizations.[22] According to Jerome Berg: "The judge cannot ignore his administrative responsibilities any more than he can his responsibility to keep abreast of the law or judge fairly the issues brought before him."[23] However, whether or not Florida's chief judges will internalize this conception of their role, even if they are given control over their support functions, is questionable.

The chief judges' failure to exercise their constitutional authority under Article V furnishes clear testimony to the fact that most judges will be reluctant administrators if further reforms are instituted. The extent to which an anti-administration bias prevails among the chief judges is reflected in their attitudes toward court clerks. Although splitting the clerks' offices would eradicate many management deficiencies, eleven judges are content to retain the status quo. A statement of one judge is particularly enlightening: "Who would take over their duties? If pure judicial clerks are appointed, I'd be responsible for training and supervising them. Who has the time? I certainly don't." The other judges who oppose alteration of the clerks' offices offered similar explanations. For example: "This idea would not change anything. Clerks are better managers than I can be"; "That's simply the work of academicians who don't understand the court system"; and "The issue is a paper tiger which has no practical foundation." Judges who are not anxious to assume the limited responsibility that would accrue to them by redefining the clerk's role may be terrified by the administrative duties prompted by reforms outlined in chapter 4. However, another conjecture is that the chief judges' desire to maintain the present arrangement of the clerks' offices is again motivated by the uncertainty surrounding that reform. Since many judges are able to maintain their judicial operations with little difficulty, the splitting of the clerks' functions is perceived as inviting unexpected troubles during what would probably be a hectic transitional period.

In order for chief judges to gain full control over the administration of their courts, they must utilize the services of their court administrators. The exigencies of the judges' judicial responsibilities demand that professionally competent assistants perform much of the administrative minutia. However, the legal profession's antipathy toward administration often influences judges' relationships with court executive assistants. Fear of bureaucratic rigidity, regimentation, and repression has motivated the judiciary in numerous states to resist professional administrators.[24] This phenomenon is especially pronounced among Florida chief judges. Court executive assistants have been relegated to ineffectual roles that resemble those of secretaries. Consequently, it may well be overly optimistic to expect chief judges to accept management assistants enthusiastically. Unless this fundamental bias can be overcome, even those judges who actively strive to provide competent administrative leadership may be so inundated by responsibilities that traditional judicial inertia will persist.

Court clerks also occupy a strategic position in the struggle to implement court reform. No other group of court managers will be more affected by attempts to standardize and centralize judicial management authority. Under a state supported judicial system, the court clerks' role will be radically altered. As locally elected officials, court clerks have a vested interest in retaining the status quo. Centralized personnel and budgetary procedures will destroy their two major sources of power: employment of large numbers of deputy clerks, and control over judicial fiscal resources in the counties. Moreover, procedural unification of the court system will deprive the clerks of their influence in form and procedure design as well as severely restrict their freedom to establish management policy. As a result, their traditional positions as independently elected politicians will be transformed into a bureaucratic version of court executive assistants. Consequently, reform represents a more immediate threat to these persons than to any other members of the judicial system. Court clerks may therefore be expected to offer the greatest resistance.

The United States Advisory Commission on Intergovernmental Relations regards elected court officials as the single greatest hindrance to judicial reform:

It is extremely difficult to abolish any public office, and these particular officials [clerks] are especially hard to eliminate. Inferior court officialdom has the habit of being extremely close to its legislature. In addition the typical clerk has numerous helpers and deputies. Where these officials are elected they have their own political organization, and usually claim a strong family, friends, and neighbors vote.[25]

These characteristics are clearly applicable to Florida's clerks: Having occupied their offices for relatively lengthy periods of time, most clerks are well-entrenched politically and enjoy favorable relationships with their legislators. In fact, approximately thirty clerks reportedly congregate in various locations throughout the state periodically to consult with legislative and judicial officials in what one judge labeled "effective lobbying efforts." The state clerks' association also employs one full-time lobbyist to argue on their behalf in Tallahassee.

A prime consideration on their lobbying agenda is reputedly "a desire to stop state encroachment." Staff reports of the Joint Select Committee on Judicial Personnel are replete with references to the arguments advanced by court clerks to "limit state encroachment into their county operation." Citing "home rule" and "local responsiveness" as justification, various groups of clerks have opposed numerous state proposals. For example, at one time or another, court clerks have clearly opposed everything from court executive assistants to centralized personnel procedures.

The court clerks' access to political powers in the state capitol and their attitudes regarding state controls are indicative of the struggle confronting reformers. Clerks represent a formidable political power in the state and thus possess a large measure of control over the direction that reform will take. The former state courts administrator described the situation thusly: "I hope we soon have a management system where clerks don't rely on political clout! As they operate now, the management area is left open and clerks simply concentrate on being clerks. This involves, in part, political pressure to maintain their functions."[26] The clerks' efforts to subvert innovation have already been successful in several selected areas and are useful in exemplifying what may well be the largest obstacle that reformers in other states will face. Through their political influence, court clerks have been able to oppose the intent of court executives, resist the splitting of most of their offices, delay attempts to implement a state personnel system, and prevent the dispersal of a study critical of their management practices.

Opposition from court clerks has been shown in this study to be a primary factor contributing to the ineffectiveness of court administrators. Traditional political relationships between chief judges and court clerks has clearly served to defeat the intent of the court executives' position. During an interview several months before the resignation of the first state courts administrator, he voiced his concern: "We administrators can't do anything unless we are given the 'key to the door' by clerks and judges. Unfortunately, neither group is yet willing to give us that key, especially the clerks."

Since the departure of the first state courts administrator, however, relationships between the court managers and central office have improved. Informal discussions with judicial personnel in Florida indicate that these improved relations are a function of one major factor: The present administrator is not perceived to be as threatening as was his predecessor. His reform recommendations are apparently less inflammatory to local judicial officials, and the person is said to be following a *gradual*[27] process of reform that is less likely to offend the present court managers.

The fact that only three counties have divided the clerks' office in accordance with Article V, Section 16 of the Florida Constitution is indicative of the clerks' political influence. Despite the administrative and conceptual advantages of such an action, most clerks have retained their traditional positions. The following quote from a chief judge partially explains this phenomenon:

I'm one of maybe ten or twenty judges in the state who favors splitting the office. There may be more, but it's not healthy to admit it. It's a very "hot" political question. Clerks have a lot of influence and a lot of friends, and they can do a lot of damage if they know you're against them.

The third example of the clerks' political influence involves the proposed personnel system of the state government. In October, 1972 the Florida legislature appropriated funds for a classification study of judicial personnel at the urging of the state administrative office. A support staff for the Joint Select Committee on Judicial Personnel was employed to operationalize the study and to make recommendations to the legislature. However, although all preliminary studies have been completed, the staff's proposals are not being seriously considered. According to a member of the staff:

The clerks shot down the idea of a personnel system. All tasks have been analyzed and we're ready to operationalize the program. But the clerks have fought us every step of the way. We're afraid to make honest recommendations to the legislature because of the political nature of the suggestions, so we edit all of our reports to the committee. If we included what we really think ought to be done with the clerks, we may not be employed much longer.

When this person was asked what has enabled the clerks to be so successful in delaying the personnel system, he responded:

Besides political influence, they've performed their own lobbying campaigns inside the counties. The deputy clerks haven't been analyzed to see how they feel about a personnel system, but the feedback we get says they're scared. Apparently, the clerks have been feeding them propaganda and giving them distorted impressions about "What would happen to me?" If four thousand deputy clerks complain to the Legislature our proposals are in for a rough time.[28]

The final example of the court clerks political influence involves a paper flow study that was completed in 1975. During 1974 the Office of State Courts Administrator sponsored the exhaustive study of court clerks' offices. The conclusions of that study were extremely critical of the court clerks' management and procedural practices. Although the supreme court had apparently hoped to utilize the findings to justify uniform procedure and form design, the study itself has not been publicized or been made generally available. This phenomenon is reportedly due to a strong political effort on the part of court clerks to force the supreme court to keep the study "under wraps."

These brief accounts of the effectiveness of the clerks' political influence represent an omen to reformers. Local judicial officials are threatened by court innovation and possess requisite political power to reinforce their convictions. Because reform opposition from court clerks is supplemented by resistance from the judiciary, major systemic alterations may only be achieved through a gradual process if major conflict is to be averted.

Macro-Political Influences

Despite the dismal outlook for reform at the local level, there are a number of encouraging indicators that state officials recognize the need for a more unified judicial system. Since the adoption of Article V, various influential governmental figures have been striving to perpetuate the reform fervor initiated by judicial reorganization. Most of their efforts have been directed toward implementation of a unitary financing system for the entire court structure. Assumption of all court operational costs by the state government is recognized as being the crucial step in granting the judicial branch the independent status it must have to properly maintain itself. Moreover, by removing the influence of local politicians from judicial policy determinations, further reforms in procedural and personnel areas would be facilitated. Because state funding is essentially the fundamental issue in any attempt to implement comprehensive judicial reform, the obstacles and arguments that arise in opposition to it are assumed in this study to be symptomatic of resistance to other less inclusive innovations.

During the public debates over Article V, several state officials openly espoused full state funding for Florida's judicial system; for example, on numerous occasions Governor Askew repeated the assertion that Article V "presupposes a judicial system funded entirely from state revenues."[29] Perhaps the most compelling statement of this philosophy was presented to the legislature on April 9, 1973, by former Chief Justice Vassar B. Carlton. In a speech in support of Article V, he inserted the following plea:

The time has come for the Legislature to recognize that the business of our courts has a statewide impact no less significant than matters of public health, the construction of roads, or the instruction of our children. Since all our courts are integral parts of our statewide judicial machinery, the obligation of the state to bear the costs involved goes beyond the level of judges and reaches down to all the support elements within the state.[30]

Thus, the issue of state funding for Florida's judicial system appeared to have been settled upon the adoption of Article V. According to all recorded legislative debates preceding the state referendum that eventually endorsed the measure, the framers and advocates of Article V clearly included the proposition that its passage would "provide much needed tax relief to the property owners by fully funding the new statewide court system."[31]

To this end, on April 4, 1972, three amendments to House Bill 4469 mandating state assumption of all court salaries and expenses, exclusive of facilities and equipment, were passed by the House. This action was predicated on the general belief that a truly uniform court system should include full state funding as an essential component in order to insure the equitable distribution of resources required for the fair administration of justice in Florida.[32] These amendments were altered to continue contributions from local funding sources in the absence of state appropriations.[33] When the provisions for state funding ultimately failed, reform proponents marshalled sufficient legislative support to achieve acceptance of an alternate proposal. Specifically, the Joint Select Committee on Judicial Personnel was created for the purpose of collecting data on the feasibility and eventual impact of state funding for all judicial personnel. The most convincing and damaging argument against adoption of the original state funding bill was that no accurate prediction of its fiscal impact could be formulated at the time. Consequently, by operationalizing an impact study, court reformers hoped to strengthen their future position.

Despite these initial (and continuing) bursts of support, unitary financing of the judicial system remains a remote possibility. The staff has submitted favorable reports regarding the feasibility of state funding, yet no legislative action is evident. In the interim between 1972 and 1977 several objections have been raised concerning the concept of a centralized judicial branch. Adversaries of state funding give the following reasons for their opposition: (1) local responsiveness will be reduced; (2) costs will increase; and (3) county officials will surrender a large measure of their authority.

An argument frequently employed by chief judges and court clerks is that state controls inevitably lead to reduced local responsiveness. Centralized bureaucracies have historically been regarded as "cold" monoliths that are insensitive to the desires of citizens. Consequently, many persons feel that if management decisions are made in a distant city by unapproachable bureaucrats, citizen access will disappear and administrative abuses will increase. Moreover, local officials are clearly apprehensive that uniform procedures may ignore local conditions and requirements: This occurrence might discourage local financial contributions toward the provision of support and other ancillary services.[34]

State assumption of judicial funding responsibilities is often regarded as economically impractical and unjustifiable. "Bigness" is normally associated with "expensiveness." A sizable bureaucracy would necessarily be established to administer budgetary and personnel systems. In every court additional staff members would probably be required to prepare budget analyses, evaluations, audits, and justifications, which, in turn, would generate a large number of records and excess paperwork. Salaries would probably increase under standard-ized personnel procedures, and additional fringe benefits would result. Moreover, in order to achieve procedural consistency, large numbers of professionally competent administrators would have to be employed. All of these factors are potential cost "increasers" for judicial operations. Although reformers contend that savings from increased efficiency will offset these higher costs, adversaries of state funding are not convinced.

A charge that cannot rationally be denied by advocates of state funding is that centralization will partially diminish county authority over the judicial system. While local officials often "take refuge" in a philosophical debate over the relative merits of state versus local control, raw political power is often actually the primary issue: Who will exercise ultimate budget and personnel authority—court clerks or centrally located judicial administrators? Counties in some states such as Colorado and North Carolina have ignored this issue and have become leaders in the movement for state court funding. The expanding demands and competition for government resources have strained local revenue sources to such an extent that state assumption of judicial costs is welcomed.[35] However, many counties in Florida operate their courts at a profit. Shifting these excess revenues to the state government represents a political problem of immense proportions. Also, Florida has been negligent in investigating funding styles that do not automatically result in a loss of local input into the budget policy process.

In addition to the political arguments that have been raised in opposition to state funding, two practical limitations exist that may complicate its implemen-tation. First, determining which agencies and services comprise the judicial system is difficult. Second, state funding may result in an underfinanced court structure.

Before state funding is implemented, a number of prior decisions must be made regarding which functions and services should be included in a consoli-dated budget.[36] For example, probation and parole commissions, juvenile officers, and bailiffs all perform functions that are directly related to the courts. State governments must therefore decide what proportion of these services is purely "judicial" in order to allocate funds properly.[37] Moreover, a great deal of controversy has arisen over the recording functions of court clerks. According to Article V, recording functions apparently belong not to the judiciary, but to the county.[38] Yet many state authorities argue that recording ought to be court funded.[39] Determining the percentage of support functions that are "judicial" as opposed to "county" thus involves further conflicts that must be resolved before state funding proposals can be seriously considered.

Another major problem of judicial system "definition" involves the locus of authority. State support will naturally result in greater state control over the judicial system. Authority to establish management priorities must be situated in a centralized office. Yet disagreement exists over which governmental agencies (or branches) should exercise this increased power. The judicial system does not presently possess sufficient administrative machinery to manage its own personnel and budgetary systems. Therefore, before a uniform judicial structure can be implemented, state authorities must either establish adequate administrative capabilities in the Office of State Courts Administrator or be prepared to burden existing agencies with increased responsibilities.

Courts funded by state governments will not necessarily receive more resources than they did under traditional financial arrangements. In fact, state government may be unable to maintain the levels of fiscal support currently provided through political relationships with local officials. According to Edward E. Pringle, it is unrealistic to assume that the court system will get everything it thinks it needs to maintain adequate operations; "the court system must expect to take its fiscal lumps along with everyone else."[40]

This phenomenon is accentuated by several additional factors. First, other than the organized bar, courts do not possess active constituencies that are useful in pressuring the legislature for increased appropriations. Thus, state agencies with interest-group support have a distinct advantage in the competition for funds. Second, judges may allow the "independent" status to discourage direct lobbying efforts with legislators. If this should occur, the court system will be "at the mercy" of appropriations committees that may be ignorant of judicial system operations.[41] Third, there are numerous judicial activities, such as jury trials, for which predicting the amount of money required for support is difficult.[42] Finally, unless the constitutional anomaly of executive review of the judicial budget is abolished, the judicial system will be extremely susceptible to antagonistic governors. If the executive officer is not cooperative, the judicial branch of government could conceivably be stripped of its operational integrity.[43]

Summary

While initiating change in any social institution is normally a slow and agonizing process, sustaining that change often proves to be even more difficult. The legal system is perhaps the most static institution in American society and thus is particularly resistant to innovation. Tradition, precedent, and an element of sacredness impart to the judicial system an aversion to any alteration in its structures, procedures, or methods of operation. Reformers who attempt to modernize the courts through administrative practices are confronted by further obstacles. Law and administration are regarded as mutually contradictory concepts by many members of the legal profession. Law emphasizes precedent and assiduous attention to procedures designed to insure "justice," while administration is more concerned with efficiency and economy. As a result, many court reforms are regarded as assaults on fundamental legal precepts and doctrines.

Two other major factors threaten to obstruct the specific reforms proposed for Florida's judicial system in chapter 4. Vested interests of chief judges and court clerks are endangered by centralization of personnel and budget systems. Judges are fearful that their independence will be usurped by state agencies and are unwilling to abandon traditional modes of operation. Court clerks object to the abolition of their independent authority and have demonstrated that they possess adequate political influence to alter the course of reform.

Moreover, there are numerous arguments that may legitimately be advanced against state assumption of judicial budget and personnel responsibilities. Reduced local responsiveness, cost increases, and loss of local autonomy may all result from state controls. While testing the validity of these objections is impossible without implementing the advocated reforms, they have many adherents in state and local government and thus may prove to be insurmountable obstacles.

6 Conclusion

Both the actual state of reform in Florida and the "solutions" offered herein for the remaining dilemmas depart from the conventional wisdom of Roscoe Pound and the American Bar Association *Standards*. As is suggested by the contingency theorists, no absolute prescriptions can be be expected to succeed. Reforms must be designed as responses to specific and unique problems within equally unique environmental settings. While many state judicial systems are burdened by similar management difficulties, judicial actors, and political obstacles, each differs sufficiently to require individualized attention and treatment.

Court clerks are the critical variable in Florida. Indeed, they may *become* the critical variable in numerous other states as well, including Missouri[1] and Illinois.[2] The single greatest requirement for uniformity or reform in Florida is the elimination of the court clerks' influence from judicial operations. Few steps toward consistency or uniformity will be taken until this goal is accomplished. Court clerks exercise such a large amount of control and political power within the system that assuming that any major movement toward uniformity is possible without their compliance is totally unrealistic. Chief judges have been unable to assert their authority due to the inexorable link between judicial resources and the court clerks.

Despite the management dilemmas that are attributed to localistic and parochial court clerks, their resistance to the unification effort in Florida is beneficial in at least one respect. Their objections to increased state control serve to emphasize the reality that a totally centralized court system is inappropriate for Florida's economic, geographical, and judicial composition. As antagonists of centralization have argued elsewhere, administrative efficiency and effectiveness may be achieved in a nominally decentralized system.[3] The diverse nature of Florida's people, the geographic size of the state, and the varying legal needs of its citizens indicate that total state control may indeed be unnecessary, if not unwise. Numerous state officials, judges, and private citizens have acknowledged this reality. The former state courts administrator succinctly stated this philosophy in the following assertion during an interview with the author: "We need decentralization, participation; let the man who makes the decision have the authority to do so. Don't use a 1930s Harvard Business School concept of administration."

A paradox is thus evident. Local control over judicial functions is the primary cause of court system inefficiencies, yet it is strongly valued and, in the opinions of most Florida authorities, it should be preserved. A management system must therefore be devised that offers both central accountability and local responsibility and responsiveness. The only practicable alterations in Florida's judicial system must incorporate the advantages of both unification and decentralization.

The management system that is potentially most effective in reconciling the need for uniformity with the desire for local control is an analogue of Management-by-Objectives (MBO). MBO is an administrative technique that has achieved incredible popularity in the public sector within the past twenty years.[4] MBO systems function according to one major precept: Broad organizational goals and performance measures should be established centrally, and the actual achievement of the centrally derived goals should be the province of decentralized managers. In addition, MBO systems incorporate a "coaching" mentality in that goals and performance measures are not dictatorially applied but are established in concert with all responsible participants.

As applied to the Florida judicial system, a hybrid form of MBO would incorporate several components of a "unified" system, but would also employ numerous decentralized management practices. The elements of unification that are most critically needed in Florida are state funding, state personnel controls, and consistent procedural and paper flow practices established by the Florida Supreme Court. These reform components are necessary to insure uniformity where uniformity is most desirable: in the equitable distribution of resources, the quality of personnel, and the elimination of inconsistent, overlapping and dysfunctional procedures. These reforms are also the most expedient methods of eliminating the court clerks' influence in judicial operations. According to the Advisory Commission on Intergovernmental Relations, some degree of centralization is imperative because few judicial authorities are "prepared to accept a high degree of responsiveness to local needs if it means uneven and inequitable application of the law between jurisdictions."[5]

State funding, as distinguished from unitary budgeting, is very compatible with this "MBO" depiction of court administration.[6] Under a system of state financing the central authority funds the courts, but it does not necessarily exercise absolute control over administrative and fiscal operations. Judicial authorities in each region, or circuit, assume the initiative for establishing budget priorities. The central budgeting office's task of compiling and weighing the competing claims from the various regions would be eased by the use of a budgeting formula. Moreover, regional, as opposed to county, budget preparation and submittal would greatly alleviate the present confusion that exists in regard to funding levels, auditing procedures, and the like.

By establishing the circuits as regional court systems that are administratively cohesive units,[7] the archaic relationships between counties and courts could be positively modified. A similar degree of decentralization may be gained within a system of centrally derived procedural guidelines. If the "central administration concentrates upon establishing appropriate standards of performance" and leaves most of the "detail of achieving those standards to the individual courts,"[8] consistency, accountability, and responsibility are made possible within a decentralized institutional framework. Emphasis on regional control is thus not at all incompatible with the trend toward unification.[9] Regional chief judges would assume functional responsibility for applying centrally derived standards and practices. Chief judges and their court administrators would be given enough latitude to tailor individual responses to unique regional problems. Accountability would be insured by requiring that major procedural and operational variations be approved by the central authority. In this manner the benefits of local responsiveness would be maintained; yet the problems of the present system could be effectively eliminated.

Local input into the administrative process can be assured through three subsidiary mechanisms: the use of judicial councils and committees, regional selection of court managers, and regionally supervised personnel systems. State and regional judicial councils should be established to assist the supreme court in establishing broad organizational policies. Functioning primarily as advisory bodies, these mechanisms might be supplemented through the utilization of a judicial committee system. Such committees have been useful in other states in making specific recommendations regarding certain substantive issues, such as juvenile and probate procedures, form design, jury management, and the like.[10] Input from these judicial groups would partially obviate the tendency of the supreme court to implement overly specific, cumbersome, and rigidified procedures. Moreover, they would impart an element of collegiality to the administrative process that is essential in a professional organization.[11]

Local selection of court administrators, chief judges, and court clerks is contradictory to most reform proposals. For example, Standard 9.3 of the National Advisory Commission on Criminal Justice Standards and Goals states that "local trial court administrators and regional administrators should be appointed by the state court administrator."[12] Similar recommendations frequently assert that chief judges should be appointed by the chief justice of the state supreme court. The fact that most states do not select court administrators and chief judges centrally is significant.[13] While central selection insures loyalty to state directives and procedures, the responsiveness of the court managers to their immediate superiors and/or colleagues is reduced. It is imperative that local administrators be selected by their respective chief judges (or by all the judges in the region, collectively). To do otherwise is to invite resistance that may ultimately strip professional administrators of any significant role in judicial operations. In addition, it is not likely that centrally appointed presiding judges will receive the cooperation and support of their colleagues, nor will they likely be perceived as being more responsive to the regions than to the central administration.

Finally, local input is provided for through regional supervision of judicial personnel. The establishment of a formal judicial personnel system does not presuppose that state authorities will control all facets of personnel activities. Consistent standards for employee classification, compensation, training, hiring, firing, and fringe benefits should be prepared by judicial personnel specialists within the Office of State Courts Administrator. Application of these standards, and regional variations, can be accomplished within the regional administrators' offices. This technique further insures that the local judicial system will maintain a degree of independent integrity and will not become the servant of state officials.

The trend toward decentralization in most government organizations is pronounced. There is reason to believe that such a management style is equally applicable to judicial bureaucracies. Before decentralization, however, the Florida judicial system must be purged of its most archaic elements. Assertive steps toward unification must be taken before an effective decentralized management network can be operationalized. By synthesizing the "best" elements of two competing philosophies, Florida's courts may emerge as a truly reformed, if not uniform, judicial structure.

Appendixes

Appendix A
Selected Sections of
Article V

SECTION 1. Courts.

The judicial power shall be vested in a supreme court, district courts of appeal, circuit courts and county courts. No other courts may be established by the state, any political subdivision or any municipality. The legislature shall, by general law, divide the state into appellate court districts, and judicial circuits following county lines. Commissions established by law, or administrative officers or bodies may be granted quasi-judicial power in matters connected with the functions of their offices.

SECTION 2. Administration; practice and procedure.

(a) The supreme court shall adopt rules for the practice and procedure in all courts including the time for seeking appellate review, the administrative supervision of all courts, the transfer to the court having jurisdiction, of any proceeding when the jurisdiction of another court has been improvidently invoked, and a requirement that no cause shall be dismissed because an improper remedy has been sought. These rules may be repealed by general law enacted by two-thirds vote of the membership of each house of the legislature.

(b) The chief justice of the supreme court shall be chosen by a majority of the members of the court. He shall be the chief administrative officer of the judicial system. He shall have the power to assign justices or judges, including consenting retired justices or judges, to temporary duty in any court for which the judge is qualified and to delegate to a chief judge of a judicial circuit the power to assign judges for duty in his respective circuit.

(c) A chief judge for each district court of appeal shall be chosen by a majority of the judges thereof or, if there is no majority, by the chief justice. The chief judge shall be responsible for the administrative supervision of the court.

(d) A chief judge in each circuit shall be chosen from among the circuit judges as provided by supreme court rule. The chief judge shall be responsible for the administrative supervision of the circuit courts and county courts in his circuit.

SECTION 3. Supreme court.

(a) ORGANIZATION. The supreme court shall consist of seven justices. Five justices shall constitute a quorum. The concurrence of four justices shall be necessary to a decision. When recusals for cause would prohibit the court from convening because of the requirements of this section, judges assigned to temporary duty may be substituted for justices.

(c) CLERK AND MARSHAL. The supreme court shall appoint a clerk and a marshal who shall hold office during the pleasure of the court and perform such duties as the court directs. Their compensation shall be fixed by general law. The marshal shall have the power to execute the process of the court throughout the state, and in any county may deputize the sheriff or a deputy sheriff for such purpose.

SECTION 4. District courts of appeal.

(a) ORGANIZATION. There shall be a district court of appeal serving each appellate district. Each district court of appeal shall consist of at least three judges. Three judges shall consider each case and the concurrence of two shall be necessary to a decision.

(c) CLERKS AND MARSHALS. Each district court of appeal shall appoint a clerk and a marshal who shall hold office during the pleasure of the court and perform such duties as the court directs. Their compensation shall be fixed by general law. The marshal shall have the power to execute the process of the court throughout the territorial jurisdiction of the court, and in any county may deputize the sheriff or a deputy sheriff for such purpose.

SECTION 5. Circuit courts.

(a) ORGANIZATION. There shall be a circuit court serving each judicial circuit.

(b) JURISDICTION. The circuit courts shall have original jurisdiction not vested in the county courts and jurisdiction of appeals when provided by general law. They shall have the power to issue writs of mandamus, quo warranto, certiorari, prohibition and habeas corpus, and all writs necessary or proper to the complete exercise of their jurisdiction. Jurisdiction of the circuit court shall be uniform throughout the state. They shall have the power of direct review of administrative action prescribed by general law.

SECTION 6. County courts.

(a) ORGANIZATION. There shall be a county court in each county. There shall be one or more judges for each county court as prescribed by general law.

(b) JURISDICTION. The county courts shall exercise the jurisdiction prescribed by general law. Such jurisdiction shall be uniform throughout the state.

SECTION 7. Specialized divisions.

All courts except the supreme court may sit in divisions as may be established by general law. A circuit or county court may hold civil and criminal trials and hearings in any place within the territorial jurisdiction of the court as designated by the chief judge of the circuit.

SECTION 8. Eligibility.

No person shall be eligible for office of justice or judge of any court unless he is an elector of the state and resides in the territorial jurisdiction of his court.

No justice or judge shall serve after attaining the age of seventy years except upon temporary assignment or to complete a term, one-half of which he has served. No person is eligible for the office of justice of the supreme court or judge of a district court of appeal unless he is, and has been for the preceding ten years, a member of the bar of Florida. No person is eligible for the office of circuit judge unless he is, and has been for the preceding five years, a member of the bar of Florida. Unless otherwise provided by general law, a county court judge must be a member of the bar of Florida.

SECTION 9. Determination of number of judges.

The supreme court shall establish by rule uniform criteria for the determination of the need for additional judges except supreme court justices, the necessity for decreasing the number of judges and for increasing, decreasing or redefining appellate districts and judicial circuits. If the supreme court finds that a need exists for increasing or decreasing the number of judges or increasing, decreasing or redefining appellate districts and judicial circuits, it shall, prior to the next regular session of the legislature, certify to the legislature its findings and recommendations concerning such need. Upon receipt of such certificate, the legislature, at the next regular session, shall consider the findings and recommendations and may reject the recommendations or by law implement the recommendations in whole or in part; provided the legislature may create more judicial offices than are recommended by the supreme court or may decrease the number of judicial offices by a greater number than recommended by the court only upon a finding of two-thirds of the membership of both houses of the legislature, that such a need exists. A decrease in the number of judges shall be effective only after the expiration of a term. If the supreme court fails to make findings as provided above when need exists, the legislature may by concurrent resolution request the court to certify its findings and recommendations and upon the failure of the court to certify its findings for nine consecutive months, the legislature may, upon a finding of two-thirds of the membership of both houses of the legislature that a need exists, increase or decrease the number of judges or increase, decrease or redefine appellate districts and judicial circuits.

SECTION 10. Election and terms.

(a) ELECTION. All justices and judges shall be elected by vote of the qualified electors within the territorial jurisdiction of their respective courts.

(b) TERMS. The terms of all justices of the supreme court, judges of district courts of appeal and circuit judges shall be for six years. The terms of judges of county courts shall be for four years.

SECTION 11. Vacancies.

(a) The governor shall fill each vacancy in judicial office by appointing for a term ending on the first Tuesday after the first Monday in January of the year following the next primary and general election, one of not fewer than three persons nominated by the appropriate judicial nominating commission. An election shall be held to fill that judicial office for the term of the office beginning at the end of the appointed term. The nominations shall be made within thirty days from the occurrence of a vacancy unless the period is extended by the governor for a time not to exceed thirty days. The governor must make the appointment within sixty days after the nominations have been certified to him.

(b) There shall be a separate judicial nominating commission as provided by general law for the supreme court, each district court of appeal, and each judicial circuit for all trial courts within the circuit.

SECTION 12. Discipline; removal and retirement.

(a) There shall be a judicial qualifications commission composed of:

(1) Two judges of district courts of appeal selected by the judges of those courts, two circuit judges selected by the judges of the circuit courts and two judges of county courts selected by the judges of those courts;

(2) Two electors who reside in the state, who are members of the bar of Florida, and who shall be chosen by the governing body of the bar of Florida; and

(3) Five electors who reside in the state, who have never held judicial office or been members of the bar of Florida, and who shall be appointed by the governor.

(b) The members of the judicial qualifications commission shall serve staggered terms, not to exceed six years as prescribed by general law. No member of the commission except a justice or judge shall be eligible for state judicial office so long as he is a member of the commission and for a period of two years thereafter. No member of the commission shall hold office in a political party or participate in any campaign for judicial office or hold public office; provided that a judge may participate in his own campaign for judicial office and hold that office. The commission shall elect one of its members as its chairman.

(c) The supreme court shall adopt rules regulating proceedings of the commission, the filing of vacancies by the appointing authorities and the temporary replacement of disqualified or incapacitated members. After a recommendation of removal of any justice or judge, the record of the proceedings before the commission shall be made public.

(d) Upon recommendation of two-thirds of the members of the judicial qualifications commission, the supreme court may order that the justice or judge be disciplined by appropriate reprimand, or be removed from office with termination of compensation for willful or persistent failure to perform his duties or for other conduct unbecoming a member of the judiciary, or be involuntarily retired for any permanent disability that seriously interferes with the performance of his duties. After the filing of a formal proceeding and upon request of the commission, the supreme court may suspend the justice or judge from office, with or without compensation, pending final determination of the inquiry.

(e) The power of removal conferred by this section shall be both alternative and cumulative to the power of impeachment and to the power of suspension by the governor and removal by the senate.

SECTION 13. Prohibited activities.

All justices and judges shall devote full time to their judicial duties. They shall not engage in the practice of law or hold office in any political party.

SECTION 14. Judicial salaries.

All justices and judges shall be compensated only by state salaries fixed by general law. The judiciary shall have no power to fix appropriations.

SECTION 15. Attorneys; admission and discipline.

The supreme court shall have exclusive jurisdiction to regulate the admission of persons to the practice of law and the discipline of persons admitted.

SECTION 16. Clerks of the circuit courts.

There shall be in each county a clerk of the circuit court who shall be selected pursuant to the provisions of Article VIII section 1. Notwithstanding any other provision of the constitution, the duties of the clerk of the circuit court may be divided by special or general law between two officers, one serving as clerk of court and one serving as ex officio clerk of the board of county commissioners, auditor, recorder, and custodian of all county funds. There may be a clerk of the county court if authorized by general or special law.

Appendix B
Position Description:
Court Administrators

The following is the official position description of circuit court administrators in the State of Florida. This description emanates from the Office of State Courts Administrator.

Function

This officer must perform his supervisory and management function at both the circuit court and the county court levels. His chief judge, as the chief administrative officer of all courts within the circuit, has complete management responsibility for each county court in the circuit. The administrator, therefore, can be expected to be required to divide his efforts between the circuit court and the county court levels.

    —Performs court administrative duties of a nonjudicial nature to relieve the chief judge of the circuit court of various administrative and management functions in his capacity as the chief administrative officer of the circuit.

Examples of Work Performed

—Maintains a central circuit office for administrative services and assistance on behalf of all courts and court personnel in the circuit and employs such staff as necessary to assist him in the efficient performance of his duties.

    —Serves as executive assistant to the chief judge of the circuit court by providing for the administrative needs of the circuit court and county courts in the circuit.

    —Establishes and maintains a management information system effecting liaison and coordination among the courts and judges of the judicial circuit.

    —Considers and evaluates the business of the courts and means of improving and administration of justice within the judicial system of the circuit.

    —Formulates and submits to the chief judge recommendations for continuing improvements of the judicial system.

    —Collects, compiles and analyzes statistical data and other information on the work of other offices related to and serving the courts, and submits to the chief judge and the circuit court periodic reports with respect thereto.

    —Is responsible for the collection of data required for the uniform case reporting system by the Office of the State Courts Administrator and for the liaison activities involved in the expansion of that system to a total state-wide management information system.

—Collects and compiles information on courtrooms, offices and other facilities of the courts and submits recommendations to the chief judge and the circuit court with respect thereto.

—Assigns clerks and bailiffs; regulates use of courtrooms; provides specialized or technical services to members of the judicial circuit in connection with management-information systems used in the jurisdiction.

—Examines the condition of the dockets and the practice and procedures of the courts and makes recommendations to the chief judge and the circuit court for expediting litigation.

—Assists the chief judge in the assignment of judges and in providing for the best utilization of judges and all court personnel.

—Conducts studies and research with respect to court operations on his own initiative or on request of the chief judge.

—Conducts studies and evaluations of increased and innovative uses of mechanization and computerization and makes recommendations to the court regarding the mechanization and computerization of court operations and services where feasible and desirable.

—Recommends such changes in organization, operation, and procedures of the court which are appropriate for court rule and which will improve the administration of the judicial system.

—Prepares and submits an annual report on the work of the courts within the circuit and on the activities of the office of the administrator.

—Represents the chief judge of the judicial circuit in meetings with members of the press and government, political, civic and other leaders on assigned matters and/or on his own initiative.

—Represents the courts in his circuit in exchanges with the Office of the State Courts Administrator.

—Provides executive direction to one or more major divisions of the circuit court.

—Examines and reports to the chief judge at regular intervals on the status of persons charged with crime.

—Coordinates engagements, travel itinerary, and other commitments of the chief judge in performance of his administrative or other judicial duties.

—Represents the chief judge of the judicial circuit in the processing and approval of correspondence in areas of assigned responsibility.

—Responsible for the courts' budget and for budgeting process.

—Performs such additional duties as may be assigned him by the chief judge of the circuit court.

Required Skills, Knowledge, and Abilities

—Knowledge of the legal processes involved in civil and criminal litigation; knowledge of clerical procedures incidental to the operation of civil and criminal courts; knowledge of the business and professional relationships and ethics involved among courts, judges, attorneys, and law enforcement agencies.

—Skill in the principles of administration, office management and systems analysis.

—Ability to work smoothly and efficiently in a cooperative atmosphere with the judges, attorneys, court officers, public officials, and administrative staffs functioning within the judicial circuit.

—Ability to develop and implement administrative procedures.

—Ability to prepare and submit concise reports in both oral and written form.

—Ability to elicit the cooperation and confidence of the practitioners within the system he serves.

Minimum Training and Experience

—Graduation from an accredited four-year college or university and four years experience in the area of specialization or six years executive administrative management experience at a comparable level of responsibility. Postgraduate study in the field of public administration, business administration or judicial administration can be substituted for three years of the minimum experience required. Postgraduate study in law can be substituted for two years of the minimum experience required. In those circuits of twenty judges or less the following additional qualifications are required:

- —masters degree in the field of public administration, business administration or judicial administration and a certificate from a nationally recognized institute for court management; the certificate is not required if the masters degree is in judicial administration, *or*
- —twelve years executive administrative management experience at a comparable level of responsibility and the certificate as set forth above.

Appendix C
Statutory Duties of
Chief Judges

According to *Florida Statutes*, Chapter 43.26, chief judges shall exercise the following powers:

(1) The presiding judge of each judicial circuit, who shall be a circuit judge, shall exercise administrative supervision over all the trial courts within the judicial circuit except municipal courts and over the judges and other officers of such courts.

(2) The presiding judge of the circuit shall have the power:

(a) To assign judges to the trial of civil or criminal cases, to preliminary hearings, or to divisions and to determine the length of the assignment;
(b) To assign clerks and bailiffs;
(c) To regulate use of courtrooms;
(d) To supervise dockets and calendars;
(e) To require attendance of prosecutors and public defenders; and
(f) To do everything necessary to promote the prompt and efficient administration, of justice in the courts over which he presides.

(3) The presiding judge shall be responsible to the chief justice of the supreme court for such information as may be required by the chief justice, including but not limited to, caseload, status of dockets, and disposition of cases in the courts over which he presides.

(4) The presiding judge of the circuit shall be selected by a majority of the judges subject to this section in that circuit for a term of two years. The presiding judge may succeed himself for successive terms.

(5) Failure of any judge, clerk, prosecutor, public defender, or other officer of the court to comply with an order or directive of the presiding judge under this section shall constitute neglect of duty for which such officer may be suspended from office as provided by law.

(6) There may be an executive assistant to the presiding judge who shall perform such duties as the presiding judge may direct.

Notes

Notes

Chapter 1
Introduction

1. For a related discussion, see Larry C. Berkson, Steven W. Hays, and Susan J. Carbon (eds.), *Managing the State Courts* (St. Paul: West Publishing, 1977), pp. 1-3.

2. See, e.g., Herbert Jacob, *Justice in America* (Boston: Little, Brown, 1972), pp. 152-63; and Richard J. Richardson and Kenneth N. Vines, *The Politics of Federal Courts* (Boston: Little, Brown, 1970), pp. 48-54.

3. See, e.g., Leonard Downie, Jr., *Justice Denied* (Baltimore: Penguin Books, 1972); and Jerome Frank, *Courts on Trial: Myth and Reality in American Justice* (New York: Atheneum, 1971).

4. For a complete discussion, see James A. Gazell, "Judicial Management at the State Level: Its Neglect, Growth, and Principal Facets," *California Western Law Review* 7 (Spring 1971):355-82.

5. The most comprehensive and recent of these proposals is included in, American Bar Association Commission on Standards of Judicial Administration, *Standards Relating to Court Organization* (Chicago: American Bar Association, 1974).

6. Larry Berkson and Steven W. Hays, "Injecting Court Administrators Into an Old System: A Case of Conflict in Florida," *Justice System Journal* 2 (Spring 1976):57.

7. David J. Saari, "Management and Courts: A Perplexing Nexus," *American University Law Review* 20 (December 1970-March 1971):604.

8. Roscoe Pound, "The Causes of Popular Dissatisfaction with the Administration of Justice," *Journal of the American Judicature Society* 20 (February 1937):178-87.

9. Mary L. Volcansek, "Conventional Wisdom of Court Reform," in Berkson, Hays, and Carbon (eds.), *Managing the State Courts*, pp. 18-23.

10. President's Commission on Law Enforcement and the Administration of Justice, *Task Force Report: The Courts* (Washington, D.C.: Government Printing Office, 1967), pp. 92-6.

11. American Bar Association, *Standards*.

12. For a thorough comparison of various reform proposals, see Allan Ashman and Jeffrey A. Parness, "The Concept of a Unified Court System," *DePaul Law Review* 24 (Fall 1974):1-41.

13. Ibid., p. 16.

14. There are numerous aspects of reform over which scholars disagree. See, e.g., Steven W. Hays, "Contemporary Trends in Court Unification," in Berkson, Hays, and Carbon (eds.), *Managing the State Courts*, pp. 122-31.

15. Frank, *Courts on Trial.*

16. See, e.g., Herbert Jacob, *Debtors in Court* (Chicago: Rand McNally, 1969); James Eisenstein and Herbert Jacob, *Felony Justice* (Boston: Little, Brown, 1977); and David W. Neubauer, *Criminal Justice in Middle America* (Morristown, N.J.: General Learning Press, 1974).

17. See, e.g., James R. Klonoski and Robert I. Mendelsohn, *The Politics of Local Justice* (Boston: Little, Brown, 1971); and Stephen Wasby, "Public Law, Politics, and the Local Courts," *Journal of Public Law* 16 (1965):105-30.

18. James A. Gazell, "State Trial Courts: An Odyssey Into Faltering Bureaucracies," *San Diego Law Review* 8 (March 1971):275-332.

19. Ibid.

20. Edward B. McConnell, "The Role of the State Court Administrator," in *Justice in the States*, addresses to the National Conference on the Judiciary, March 11-14, 1971, Law Enforcement Assistance Administration, Washington, D.C., 1971, pp. 89-90.

21. Ernest C. Friesen, Jr., Edward C. Gallas, and Nesta M. Gallas, *Managing the Courts* (Indianapolis: Bobbs-Merrill, 1971); Dorothy W. Nelson (ed.), *Judicial Administration and the Administration of Justice* (St. Paul: West Publishing, 1974); H. Ted Rubin, *The Courts: Fulcrum of the Justice System* (Pacific Palisades, Calif.: Goodyear Publishing, 1976); and Russell R. Wheeler and Howard R. Whitcomb (eds.), *Judicial Administration* (Englewood Cliffs, N.J.: Prentice-Hall, 1977).

22. James A. Gazell, *State Trial Courts as Bureaucracies* (New York: Dunnellen Publishing, 1975), p. 45.

23. For an excellent discussion of this phenomenon as it occurs in other organizations, see Victor A. Thompson, *Modern Organizations* (New York: Alfred A. Knopf, 1961).

24. *Fifth Report of the Special Committee on Study of the Judicial System, The Bar Bulletin* 43 (1938):113, as quoted in Jerome S. Berg, "Assumption of Administrative Responsibility by the Judiciary," *Suffolk University Law Review* 6 (Summer 1972):806.

25. Lynn W. Jensen and Francis E. Dosal, "Circuit Clerks' Study," *State Court Journal* 1 (Summer 1977):17-21.

26. Ralph R. Temple, "Court Officers: Their Selection and Responsibility," *New York University Law Quarterly Review* 22 (Spring 1947):401-32.

27. Richardson and Vines, *The Politics of Federal Courts*, p. 52.

28. Richard W. Gable, "Modernizing Court Administration: The Case of the Los Angeles Superior Court," *Public Administration Review* 31 (March-April 1971):133-43.

29. Larry C. Berkson, "The Emerging Ideal of Court Unification," *Judicature* 60 (March 1977):372-82.

30. James A. Gazell, "Lower Court Unification in the American States," *Arizona State Law Journal* (1974):677.

131

31. Barbara Schulert and Bill Hoelzel, "Court Reform," *Judicature* 60 (January 1977):281-89.

32. Bill Hoelzel, "A Citizen Campaign Brings Court Reform to Wisconsin," *Judicature* 61 (June-July 1977):46-47.

33. Jeffrey Parness and Chris Korbakes, *A Study of the Procedural Rule-Making Power in the United States* (Chicago: American Judicature Society, 1973).

34. Berkson, "The Emerging Ideal," p. 377.

35. Larry C. Berkson, "Court Unification in the Fifty States," paper delivered for delivery at the annual meeting of the American Society for Public Administration, Atlanta, 1977.

36. Carl Baar, *Separate But Subservient: Court Budgeting in the American States* (Lexington, Mass.: D.C. Heath, 1975), as updated in Carl Baar, "The Limited Trend Toward Court Financing and Unitary Budgeting in the States," in Berkson, Hays, and Carbon (eds.), *Managing the State Courts*, pp. 269-80.

37. See Howell T. Heflin, "The Judicial Article Implementation Act," *Alabama Law Review* 28 (Spring 1977):215-41.

38. See Pat Chapin, "Kentucky Votes in New Court," *Judicature* 59 (January 1976):306-07.

39. Florida *Constitution*, art. V., sec. 2 (d).

40. The Honorable B.K. Roberts, as quoted in *Florida Judicial System Statistical Report* (Tallahassee: Office of the State Courts Administrator, 1973), p. 1.

41. Florida statutes define the jurisdiction thusly: "County Courts have original jurisdiction in all criminal misdemeanor cases, of all violations of municipal and county ordinances, and of all actions of law in which the matter in controversy does not exceed the sum of $2,500. Circuit Courts have exclusive jurisdiction in all felonies and of all misdemeanors arising out of felonies; of all proceedings related to probate, guardianship, incompetency, and equity; of all juvenile proceedings except traffic cases, and of all other civil cases involving amounts in excess of $2,500." See *Florida Statutes*, Chapter 72-404; *Florida Statutes*, Section 26.012.

42. *Florida Judicial System Statistical Report* (Tallahassee: Office of the State Courts Administrator, 1973), p. 5.

43. Manning J. Dauer, *Proposed Amendments to the Florida Constitution*, University of Florida Civic Information Series, No. 52 (Gainesville: Public Administration Clearing Service, 1972), pp. 1-7.

44. Manning J. Dauer and Thomas C. Marks, Jr., "Proposed Amendment Revising Florida Court Structure," in *Proposed Amendments to the Florida Constitution*, University of Florida Civic Information Series, No. 50 (Gainesville: Public Administration Clearing Service, 1970), p. 6.

45. See Larry Berkson and Steven W. Hays, "Court Clerks: The Forgotten Politicians," *University of Miami Law Review* 30 (Spring 1976):499-516.

46. See Frank S. Cheatham, Jr., "The Making of a Court Administrator," *Judicature* 60 (October 1976):128-33.

47. See James A. Gazell, "Judicial Reorganization in Michigan," *Michigan State Bar Journal* (1975):113-21.

48. Chapin, "Kentucky Votes," p. 306.

49. Malcolm M. Feeley, "Two Models of the Criminal Justice System: An Organizational Perspective," *Law and Society Review* 7 (Spring 1973):407.

50. Ibid., p. 422.

51. See, e.g., Amitai Etzioni, *A Comparative Analysis of Complex Organizations* (New York: The Free Press, 1961).

52. See, e.g., Jim R. Carrigan, "Inherent Powers and Finance," *Trial* 7 (November-December 1971):22-25.

53. The most widely quoted goal perceptions are the "due process" and "crime control" models. See Herbert Packer, *The Limits of the Criminal Sanction* (Stanford: Stanford University Press, 1968).

54. Amitai Etzioni, "Two Approaches to Organization Analysis," *Administrative Science Quarterly* 5 (June 1960):257-58.

55. Feeley, "Two Models," pp. 407-25.

56. See, e.g., Abraham Blumberg, *Criminal Justice* (Chicago: Quadrangle Books, 1967); George Cole (ed.), *Criminal Justice: Law and Politics* (New York: Duxburg Press, 1972); and Jerome Skolnick, *Justice Without Trial* (New York: John Wiley and Sons, 1966).

57. Feeley, "Two Models," p. 409.

58. Friesen, Gallas, and Gallas, *Managing the Courts*, p. 19.

59. Hays, "Contemporary Trends," p. 130.

60. See David J. Saari, "Modern Court Management: Trends in Court Organization Concepts," *Justice System Journal* 2 (Spring 1976):19-33; and Geoffrey Gallas, "The Conventional Wisdom of State Court Administration: A Critical Assessment and an Alternative Approach," *Justice System Journal* 2 (Spring 1976):35-55.

61. Hays, "Contemporary Trends," p. 130.

62. Jerome S. Berg, "The District Courts of Massachusetts," *Judicature* 59 (February 1976):344-52.

63. Claire Sellitz et al., *Research Methods in Social Relations* (New York: Holt, Rinehart, Winston, 1959), pp. 235-76.

64. See Herbert Jacob, "Black and White Perceptions of Justice," *Law and Society Review* (August 1970):69-89.

65. See Angus Campbell, *Measures of Political Attitudes* (Ann Arbor, Mich.: Survey Research Center Press, 1968).

66. See John P. Robinson, Robert Athanasiou, and Kendra B. Head, *Measures of Occupational Attitudes* (Ann Arbor, Mich.: Survey Research Center Press, 1969).

67. See Sellitz et al., *Research Methods*, pp. 255-56.

Chapter 2
The Florida Court Structure and Personnel

1. For a discussion of the tendency of states to create large numbers of special courts and for a classic discussion of other judicial problems, see Roscoe Pound, *Organization of Courts* (Boston: Little, Brown, 1940).

2. Harry O. Lawson, "Overview of Court Administration: A Commentary," paper prepared for delivery at the Institute for Court Management, American University, Washington, D.C., 1974, pp. 12-16.

3. Ibid., p. 13.

4. "1969 Report: An Historic Decade Ends," *Judicature* 53 (February 1970):270, 271.

5. This phenomenon was first characterized in such terms by Harry O. Lawson. See Lawson, "Overview of Court Administration," p. 14.

6. See Staff of the Joint Select Committee on Judicial Personnel of the Florida Legislature, "Discussion Concerning the Proposed Personnel Program," unpublished paper, Tallahassee, 1974, pp. 1-27. (Hereafter referred to as Staff Report on Proposed Personnel.)

7. For a brief discussion of the relationship between judges and elected clerks, see Ernest C. Friesen, Edward C. Gallas, and Nesta M. Gallas, *Managing the Courts* (Indianapolis: Bobbs-Merrill, 1971), pp. 16-17.

8. Staff Report on Proposed Personnel, pp. 13, 14.

9. Florida *Constitution*, art. V, sec. 2 (a).

10. Staff Report on Proposed Personnel, p. 8.

11. Barbara Schulert and Bill Hoelzel, "Court Reform," *Judicature* 60 (January 1977):286-87.

12. Florida *Constitution*, art. V, sec.

13. See, e.g., Jerome S. Berg, "Judicial Interest in Administration: The Critical Variable," *Judicature* 57 (January 1974):251-55.

14. Portions of the following data and analysis were previously published in Larry Berkson and Steven W. Hays, "Injecting Court Administrators Into An Old System: A Case of Conflict in Florida," *Justice System Journal* 2 (Spring 1976):57-76. Reprinted by permission. Much of the data was revised and updated for inclusion in this chapter.

15. Section V of Chapter 72.406 of the *Florida Statutes* states, "The Supreme Court shall develop a uniform case reporting system including a uniform means of reporting categories of cases, time required in the disposition of cases, and manner of disposition of cases." The Office of the State Courts Administrator has been given primary responsibility for operating the system that was instituted in 1973.

16. Ralph R. Temple, "Court Officers: Their Selection and Responsibilities," *New York University Law Quarterly Review* 22 (Spring 1947):406.

17. Joint Select Committee on Judicial Personnel of the Florida Legisla-

ture, "Transcript of Staff Report," unpublished paper, Tallahassee, January 13, 1975, p. 18.

18. Section 16 of Article V of the Florida *Constitution* states, "There shall in each county be a clerk of the circuit court who shall be selected pursuant to the provisions of Article VII section 1. Notwithstanding any other provisions of the constitution, the duties of the clerk of the circuit court may be divided by special or general law between two officers, one serving as clerk of the court and one serving as ex officio clerk of the board of county commissioners, auditor, recorder, and custodian of all county funds."

19. Portions of the data regarding court clerks and the accompanying analysis were previously published in Larry Berkson and Steven W. Hays, "Court Clerks: The Forgotten Politicians," *University of Miami Law Review* 30 (Spring 1976):499-516. Reprinted by permission. The material was revised for inclusion in the present chapter.

20. William C. Havard, "Notes on a Theory of State Constitutional Change: The Florida Experience," *The Journal of Politics* 21 (February 1959):85.

21. Ibid.

22. Ibid.

23. Staff Report on Proposed Personnel, p. 5.

24. For an interesting discussion of a theory of personal attitudes as they relate to policy questions, see James Q. Wilson and Edward C. Banfield, "Public Regardingness as a Value Premise," in Richard I. Hofferbert and Ira Sharkansky (eds.), *State and Urban Politics* (Boston: Little, Brown, 1971), pp. 108-49.

25. Thomas A. Henderson, "The Relative Effects of Community Complexity and of Sheriffs Upon the Professionalism of Sheriff Departments," *American Journal of Political Science* 19 (February 1975):113.

26. Ibid.

27. Harvey E. Solomon, "The Rise of the Court Executive," *Judicature* 60 (October 1976):114-18.

28. See, e.g., Fannie J. Klein, "The Position of the Trial Court Administrator in the States," *Judicature* 50 (April 1967):278-80; Arnold M. Malech, "A Glass House: Court Administration from the Inside," *Judicature* 56 (January 1973):249-51; and Bernadine Meyer, "Court Administration: The Newest Profession," *Duquesne Law Review* 10 (1971):220-35.

29. American Bar Association Commission on Standards of Judicial Administration, *Standards Relating to Court Organization* (Chicago: American Bar Association, 1974), p. 86.

30. Ibid., 87-89.

31. As quoted in Meyer, "Court Administration," p. 233.

32. *Florida Judicial System Statistical Report* (Tallahassee: Office of the State Courts Administrator, 1973), p. 6.

33. The statement that court administrators must gain "authority through competence" is attributed to Ernest C. Friesen.

34. Staff of the Joint Select Committee on Judicial Personnel of the Florida Legislature, "Position Paper on the Implementation of Article V," unpublished paper, Tallahassee, November 1, 1973, pp. 9-10.

35. Ibid., p. 10.

36. *Florida Statistical Report*, p. 6.

37. Staff Report on Proposed Personnel, pp. 8-15.

38. Ibid., p. 12.

39. Ibid., p. 8.

40. Ibid., p. 14.

Chapter 3
The Management Dilemmas

1. Larry C. Berkson, "Selection of State Judges: Election or Appointment?" in Larry C. Berkson, Steven W. Hays, and Susan J. Carbon (eds.), *Managing the State Courts* (St. Paul: West Publishing 1977), p. 135.

2. Dorothy W. Nelson, "Variations on a Theme—Selection and Tenure of Judges," in Dorothy W. Nelson (ed.), *Judicial Administration and the Administration of Justice* (St. Paul: West Publishing, 1974), p. 703.

3. Ibid.

4. Ernest C. Friesen, Edward C. Gallas, and Nesta M. Gallas, *Managing the Courts* (Indianapolis: Bobbs-Merrill, 1971), p. 3.

5. Ibid.

6. Larry C. Berkson, *A Merit Plan for Selecting Judges in Florida*, University of Florida Civic Information Series, No. 55 (Gainesville: Public Administration Clearing Service, 1975), p. 12.

7. For a related discussion, see Ernest C. Friesen, Edward C. Gallas, and Nesta M. Gallas, "The Judge's Role," in Nelson (ed.), *Judicial Administration*, pp. 873-80.

8. William C. Kandt, "The Judge as Administrator—Let Us Look at Him," *University of Kansas Law Review* 8 (March 1960):435.

9. Ibid.

10. Joint Select Committee on Judicial Personnel of the Florida Legislature, "Transcript of Staff Report," unpublished paper, Tallahassee, Florida, January 13, 1975, p. 9. The Committee actually typified the system as being composed of sixty-eight units, the extra one resulting from the inclusion of the supreme court.

11. National Center for State Courts, *Administrative Unification of the Maine State Courts* (Boston: National Center for State Courts, 1975).

12. See, e.g., Francis C. Cady, "Court Modernization: Retrospective, Prospective, and Perspective," *Suffolk University Law Review* 6 (Summer 1972):815; Jim R. Carrigan, "Inherent Powers and Finance," *Trial* 7 (November-

December 1971):22-25; and James A. Gazell, "Judicial Management at the State Level: Its Neglect, Growth, and Principal Facets," *California Western Law Review* 7 (Spring 1971):355-82.

13. See, e.g., Walter H. McLaughlin, "Of Men and Buildings—Crisis in Judicial Administration," *Massachusetts Law Quarterly* 55 (Fall 1970):331-34.

14. See, e.g., Gerald S. Blaine, "Computer-Based Information Systems Can Help Solve Urban Court Problems," *Judicature* 54 (November 1970):149-53; Robert L. Chartrand, "Systems Technology and Judicial Administration," *Judicature* 52 (December 1968):194-98; and Roy N. Freed, "Computers in Judicial Administration," *Judicature* 52 (May 1969):419-21.

15. *Draft Report on Florida Judicial Recording and Paper Flow Procedures* (Tallahassee: Office of State Courts Administrator, 1975), no pagination. (Hereafter referred to as *Draft Report*.)

16. For a related discussion, see Jerome S. Berg, "Assumption of Administrative Responsibility by the Judiciary: Rx for Reform," *Suffolk University Law Review* 6 (Summer 1972):804-06.

17. For a related discussion, see National Center for State Courts, *Administrative Unification*, 59-61.

18. See, e.g., Aaron Wildavsky, *The Politics of the Budgetary Process* (Boston: Little, Brown, 1974).

19. Geoffrey C. Hazard, Jr., as quoted in, Harry O. Lawson, "Overview of Court Administration: A Commentary," paper prepared for delivery at the Institute for Court Management, American University, Washington, D.C., 1974, p. 22.

20. See, e.g., Edward E. Pringle, "Fiscal Problems of a State Court System," paper prepared for delivery to the Conference of Chief Justices, Seattle, 1972; and Edward B. McConnell, "A Blueprint for the Development of the New Jersey Judicial System," paper prepared for delivery at the Judicial Conference of New Jersey, Newark, 1969.

21. Much of this problem arises from the fact that many facets of court financing are simply "unpredictable," such as jury expenses and witness fees. See Pringle, "Fiscal Problems."

22. Staff of the Joint Select Committee on Judicial Personnel of the Florida Legislature," "Discussion Concerning the Proposed Personnel Program," unpublished paper, Tallahassee, 1974, pp. 5-6. (Hereafter referred to as Staff Report on Proposed Personnel.)

23. *Florida Statutes*, Chapter 28.091.

24. Staff Report on Proposed Personnel, p. 6.

25. Rule 3.191 (the "Speedy Trial Rule") states that every person charged with a misdemeanor must be brought to trial within ninety days, and every felony case must be tried within one hundred eighty days. Any accused person has the option of demanding a trial in sixty days, unless the state is granted a continuance "because of exceptional circumstances."

26. Carl Baar, "The Limited Trend Toward Court Financing and Unitary Budgeting in the States," in Berkson, Hays, and Carbon (eds.), *Managing the State Courts*, p. 271.

27. *Draft Report.*

28. Ibid.

29. Ibid.

30. Interview with members of the Staff of the Joint Select Committee on Judicial Personnel of the Florida Legislature, Tallahassee, April 17, 1975.

31. Ibid.

32. *Draft Report.*

33. Ibid.

34. Ibid.

35. Ibid.

36. Joint Select Committee, "Transcript of Staff Report," p. 11.

37. Roscoe Pound, "Organization of Courts," in Nelson (ed.), *Judicial Administration*, p. 35.

38. See, e.g., Larry C. Berkson and Steven W. Hays, "The Forgotten Politicians: Court Clerks," *University of Miami Law Review* 30 (Spring 1976):499-516.

39. Staff Report on Proposed Personnel, p. 16.

40. Ibid.

41. Ibid.

42. Ibid., p. 5.

43. Jessie-Lynne Kear, "It Should Have Been as Easy as Signing Your Name," *The Florida Times-Union*, Jacksonville, June 25, 1975, p. B-11.

44. Joint Select Committee, "Transcript of Staff Report," pp. 12-13.

45. Staff of the Joint Select Committee on Judicial Personnel of the Florida Legislature, "Position Paper on the Implementation of Article V," unpublished paper, Tallahassee, November 1, 1973, pp. 3-4.

46. Staff Report on Proposed Personnel, pp. 8-9.

47. *Florida Statutes Annotated*, Chapter 216.111; Chapter 110.06.

48. For a related discussion, see Berg, "Assumption of Administrative Responsibility," pp. 796-814.

49. Staff Report on Proposed Personnel, p. 9.

50. *Florida Statutes*, Chapters 26.012, 34.01.

51. *Florida Statutes Annotated*, Chapter 26.021.

52. *Florida Statutes Annotated*, Chapter 51.011.

53. *Florida Statutes Annotated*, Chapter 83.

54. *Florida Statutes*, Chapter 318.

55. Berg, "Assumption of Administrative Responsibility," p. 805.

56. *Draft Report.*

57. Ibid.

58. Ibid.

59. Ibid.

60. Numerous authors have characterized courts as state agencies. See, e.g., Berg, "Assumption of Administrative Responsibility," p. 807.

61. Ibid., p. 808.

62. Larry C. Berkson, "Court Unification in the Fifty States," paper prepared for delivery at the annual meeting of the American Society for Public Administration, Atlanta, 1977.

63. See, e.g., James A. Gazell, "A Taxonomy of State Court Personnel Management," *St. Johns Law Review* 49 (Fall 1974):74-96; James A. Gazell, "Lower Court Unification in the American States," *Arizona State Law Journal* (1974):653-78; and James A. Gazell, "State Judicial Financing: Preliminaries, Progress, Provisions, and Prognosis," *Kentucky Law Journal* 63 (1975):73-105.

64. Jeffrey Perlman, "Orange County Clerk May Lose Most of His Duties," *Los Angeles Times*, August 26, 1977, p. II-1.

Chapter 4
Reforming the Judicial System

1. See Jerome S. Berg, "Assumption of Administrative Responsibility by the Judiciary: Rx for Reform," *Suffolk University Law Review* 6 (Summer 1972):814.

2. For contradictory arguments, see Harold H. Greene, "Court Reform: What Purpose?" *American Bar Association Journal* 58 (March 1972):247-50.

3. See, e.g., Jeremy Main, "Only Radical Reform Can Save the Courts," *Fortune* 82 (August 1970):110-54; and Alexander Smith and Harriet Pollack, *Some Sins Are Not Crimes* (New York: New Viewpoints, 1975).

4. See, e.g., William J. Campbell, "Proposals for Improvement in the Administration of Criminal Justice," *Chicago Bar Record* (November 1972):75-81; and Steven Flanders and Alan Sager, "Court Management Methods and Delay in Federal District Courts," in Russell R. Wheeler, Howard R. Whitcomb (eds.), *Judicial Administration* (Englewood Cliffs, N.J.: Prentice-Hall, 1977), pp. 226-40.

5. See, e.g., Ruggero J. Aldisert, "A Metropolitan Court Conquers its Backlog," *Judicature* 51 (January-February 1968):202-07, 247-52.

6. Staff of the Joint Select Committee on Judicial Personnel of the Florida Legislature, "Position Paper on the Implementation of Article V," unpublished paper, Tallahassee, November 1, 1973, p. 3.

7. Arthur D. Larson, "Representative Bureaucracy and Administrative Responsibility: A Reassessment," in Joseph A. Uveges, Jr. (ed.), *The Dimensions of Public Administration* (Boston: Holbrook Press, 1975), p. 543.

8. Larry C. Berkson, "Court Unification in the Fifty States," paper prepared for delivery at the annual meeting of the American Society for Public Administration, Atlanta, 1977, p. 10.

9. National Advisory Commission on Criminal Justice Standards and Goals, *The Courts* (Washington, D.C.: Government Printing Office, 1973), p. 180. The relationship between central and regional administrators and judges that is specified in these standards has been echoed in almost every other reform proposal.

10. See, e.g., National Center for State Courts, *Administrative Unification of the Maine State Courts* (Boston: National Center for State Courts, 1975), pp. 23-25.

11. James A. Gazell, *State Trial Courts as Bureaucracies* (New York: Dunellen Publishing, 1975), pp. 25-27.

12. James A. Gazell, "A Taxonomy of State Court Personnel Management," *St. Johns Law Review* 49 (Fall 1974):84.

13. Ibid.

14. For a related discussion, see National Center for State Courts, *Administrative Unification*, pp. 71-75.

15. National Advisory Commission, *The Courts*, pp. 180, 181.

16. Kenneth N. Chantry, "Effective Use of Present Resources," in *Justice in the States*, addresses to the National Conference on the Judiciary, March 11-14, 1971, Law Enforcement Assistance Administration, Washington, D.C., 1971, p. 158.

17. Joint Select Committee, "Position Paper," pp. 10, 11.

18. See, e.g., Delmar Karlen, "Judicial Education," *American Bar Association Journal* 52 (June 1966):1049-54.

19. Maurice Rosenberg, "Frank Talk on Improving the Administration of Justice," *Texas Law Review* 47 (1969):1031.

20. Ibid.

21. Larry Berkson and Lenore Haggard, "The Education and Training of Judges in the United States," in Larry C. Berkson, Steven W. Hays, and Susan J. Carbon (eds.), *Managing the State Courts* (St. Paul: West Publishing, 1977), p. 148.

22. Ibid.

23. "More Education for Judges," *Institute of Judicial Administration Report* 8 (Spring 1976):1-2.

24. Staff of the Joint Select Committee on Judicial Personnel of the Florida Legislature, "Memorandum on Staff Meeting," unpublished paper, Tallahassee, September 20, 1974, p. 5. The Staff recommended a *five*-year term.

25. Ernest C. Friesen, Jr., Edward C. Gallas, and Nesta M. Gallas, *Managing the Courts* (Indianapolis: Bobbs-Merrill, 1971), p. 140.

26. James D. Thompson, *Organizations in Action* (New York: McGraw-Hill, 1967), p. 118.

27. Luverne V. Rieke, "Unification, Funding, Discipline and Administration: Cornerstones for a New Judicial Article," *Washington Law Review* 48 (1973):831.

28. Larry C. Berkson, "Selection of State Judges: Election Or Appointment?" in Berkson, Hays, and Carbon (eds.), *Managing the State Courts*, p. 136.

29. See, e.g., Bradley C. Canon, "The Impact of Formal Selection Processes on the Characteristics of Judges—Reconsidered," in Russell R. Wheeler and Howard R. Whitcomb (eds.), *Judicial Administration* (Englewood Cliffs, N.J.: Prentice-Hall, 1977), pp. 126-38.

30. Barbara Schulert and Bill Hoelzel, "Court Reform," *Judicature* 60 (January 1977):286.

31. Although this division of responsibility appears to be a violation of the separation of powers doctrine, no court decision has challenged its legality. In fact, a 1908 Florida Supreme Court case seemingly legitimizes the present relationship between court clerks and the two branches of government. In *State v. Atlantic C.L.R.C.* (56 Fla. 617, 47 So. 969) the court stated: "The governmental powers . . . are those so defined by the constitution, or such as are inherent or so recognized by immemorial governmental usage, and which involve the exercise of primary and independent will, discretion and judgment, subject not to the control of another department, but only to the limitations imposed by the state and federal constitutions." This reasoning has enabled the court to make a distinction between the powers that cannot be transferred from one branch to another and the functions that apparently can be.

32. Larry C. Berkson and Steven W. Hays, "Court Clerks: The Forgotten Politicians," *University of Miami Law Review* 30 (Spring 1976):502.

33. Chantry, "Effective Use," p. 158.

34. For a related discussion, see National Center for State Courts, *Administrative Unification*, pp. 85-88.

35. Ibid., pp. 33-34.

36. Ibid., p. 87.

37. The arguments in favor of allowing the supreme court to appoint court clerks are as follows: Local judges may appoint personal friends or political acquaintances; the state government has more resources to recruit and select competent personnel; appointment by the supreme court would insure the clerks' loyalty to state policies; and radical change requires "new blood" that can best be provided by external recruitment.

38. See, e.g., Jerome S. Berg, "Judicial Interest in Administration: The Critical Variable," *Judicature* 57 (January 1974):251-55.

39. Joint Select Committee, "Memorandum," p. 3.

40. See, e.g., David J. Saari, *Modern Court Management: Trends in the Role of the Court Executive*, (Washington, D.C.: Law Enforcement Assistance Administration, 1970).

41. Joint Select Committee, "Memorandum," p. 3.

42. Ibid.

43. Samuel D. Conti, "The Courts: Summary and Recommendations," *State Court Journal* 1 (Spring 1977):20.

44. Gazell, "A Taxonomy," pp. 82-93.

45. Joint Select Committee, "Position Paper," p. 4.

46. Ibid.

47. See Edward E. Pringle, "Fiscal Problems of a State Court System," paper prepared for delivery to the Conference of Chief Justices, Seattle, August 11, 1972. See also, Geoffrey C. Hazard, Jr., Martin B. McNamera, and Irwin F. Sentilles, III, "Court Finance and Unitary Budgeting," *Yale Law Journal* 81 (June 1972):1286-1301; and Harry O. Lawson, "Overview of Court Administration: A Commentary," paper prepared for delivery at the Institute for Court Management, American University, Washington, D.C., 1974.

48. Hazard et al., "Court Finance," p. 1295.

49. Rieke, "Unification, Funding," p. 822.

50. Ibid.

51. Pringle, "Fiscal Problems," p. 7.

52. National Advisory Commission on Civil Disorders, "The Administration of Justice Under Emergency Conditions," *Report of the National Advisory Commission on Civil Disorders* (Washington, D.C.: Government Printing Office, 1968).

53. Pringle, "Fiscal Problems," p. 6.

54. Ibid.

55. *Draft Report on Florida Judicial Recording and Paper Flow Procedures* (Tallahassee: Office of State Courts Administrator, 1975), no pagination.

56. Pringle, "Fiscal Problems," pp. 3-4.

57. National Advisory Commission, *The Courts*, p. 176.

58. Geoffrey Hazard, Jr., Martin B. McNamera, and Irwin F. Sentilles, III, *Court Finance and Unitary Budgeting*, American Bar Association Commission on Standards of Judicial Administration (Chicago: American Bar Association, 1973), p. 8.

59. Pringle, "Fiscal Problems," p. 4.

60. Carl Baar, "The Limited Trend Toward Court Financing and Unitary Budgeting in the States," in Berkson, Hays, and Carbon (eds.), *Managing the State Courts*, pp. 269-80.

61. See Benjamin Overton, *Report to the Legislature on the State of the Judiciary*, unpublished address, Tallahassee, 1976, p. 1. Justice Overton noted that current state expenditures for the judicial system account for just under 1 percent of the total state budget. Since state funds account for approximately 35 percent of judicial expenditures, total state assumption should amount to no more than 3 percent of all state expenditures.

62. See, e.g., Hazard et al., "Court Finance"; Jim R. Carrigan, "Inherent Powers and Finance," *Trial* 7 (November-December 1971):22-25; and Jim R. Carrigan, *Inherent Powers of the Courts* (Reno: National College of the State Judiciary, 1973).

63. See, e.g., *Commonwealth ex rel. Carroll* v. *Tate*, 274 A. 2d 197 (1971).

64. Hugo Touchy, "Query: Will the Courts Use Their Inherent Powers?" *Judicature* 60 (December 1976):207.

65. See, e.g., *Leahy* v. *Farrell*, 66 A. 2d 577 (1949).

66. See, e.g., *Miller* v. *Hall, Circuit Court Lincoln County, Oregon* No. 25830 (1966).

67. *State ex rel. Weinstein* v. *St. Louis County*, 451 S.W. 2d 99 (1970).

68. *Noble County Council* v. *State ex rel. Fifner*, 125 N.E. 2d 709 (1955).

69. *In Re Courtroom and Office of the Fifth Branch Circuit Court, Milwaukee County*, 134 N.W. 490 (1912).

70. Carrigan, "Inherent Powers and Finance," p. 22.

71. Robert F. Fuquay, "The Doctrine of Separation of Powers in Florida," in Ernest R. Bartley (ed.), *Papers on Florida Administrative Law*, University of Florida Civic Information Series, No. 8 (Gainesville: Public Administration Clearing Service, 1952).

72. Ibid.

73. *Petition of the Florida Bar*, 61 So. 2d 646 (1952).

74. Fuquay, "The Doctrine," p. 58.

75. *Robbins* v. *Carlton*, 211 So. 2d 562 (1968). In this case, an Eighteenth Judicial Circuit ex parte order refusing to honor a gubernatorial appointee as official court reporter was upheld, although the court's implied powers were not cited in the reasoning.

76. Hazard et al., "Court Finance," p. 1290.

77. Ibid., pp. 1290-92.

78. Ibid.

79. National Center for State Courts, *Administrative Unification*, p. 74.

80. Ibid., p. 72.

81. Howard T. Heflin, "The Judicial Article Implementation Act," *Alabama Law Review* 28 (Spring 1977):229.

82. Staff of the Joint Select Committee on Judicial Personnel of the Florida Legislature, "Discussion Concerning the Proposed Personnel Program," unpublished paper, Tallahassee, 1974, pp. 20-26. (Hereafter referred to as Staff Report on Proposed Personnel.)

83. Ibid., pp. 22-25.

84. National Center for State Courts, *Administrative Unification*, p. 74.

85. Staff Report on Proposed Personnel, p. 19.

86. See, e.g., Berg, 'Assumption of Administrative Responsibility," p. 802.

Chapter 5
Obstacles to Reform

1. United States Advisory Commission on Inter-Governmental Relations, *Report on State-Local Relations in the Criminal Justice System* (Washington, D.C.: Government Printing Office, 1971), pp. 194-95.

2. Ibid.

3. See Goodwin Watson, "Resistance to Change," in Goodwin Watson (ed.), *Concepts for Social Change* (Newark: Institute for Applied Behavioral Sciences, 1967), pp. 10-25.

4. Herbert Jacob, *Justice in America* (Boston: Little, Brown, 1972), p. 13.

5. Ibid.

6. Ibid., p. 14.

7. Alfred F. Conrad, "The Crisis of Justice," *Washburn Law Journal* 11 (Fall 1971):3.

8. See, e.g., Thurman W. Arnold, *The Symbols of Government* (New York: Harcourt, Brace and World, 1962); and Jacob, *Justice in America*, p. 14.

9. See Ernest C. Friesen, "Constraints and Conflicts in Court Administration," *Public Administration Review* 31 (March-April 1971):121-24; and Ernest C. Friesen, Edward C. Gallas, and Nesta M. Gallas, *Managing the Courts* (Indianapolis: Bobbs-Merrill, 1971), pp. 45-65.

10. Friesen, "Constraints," p. 122.

11. Friesen et al., *Managing the Courts*, p. 48.

12. For a related discussion, see Jacob, *Justice in America*, pp. 15, 16.

13. Friesen et al., *Managing the Courts*, p. 51.

14. See, e.g., Luvern V. Rieke, "Unification, Funding, Discipline and Administration: Cornerstones for a New Judicial Article," *Washington Law Review* 48 (1973):828-31.

15. Friesen, et al., *Managing the Courts*, pp. 7, 13-14.

16. See, e.g., Nesta M. Gallas, "Court Administration: A Discipline or a Focus?" *Public Administration Review* 31 (March-April 1971):143-48.

17. For a discussion of the increasing tendency of law schools to teach administration, see James A. Gazell, "University and Law School Education in Judicial Administration: A Case of National Proliferation," *Detroit College of Law Review* (1976):423-87.

18. See, e.g., David J. Saari, "Management and Courts: A Perplexing Nexus," *American University Law Review* 20 (December 1970-March 1971):604-07.

19. Harold H. Greene, "Court Reform: What Purpose?" *American Bar Association Journal* 58 (March 1972):250.

20. See, e.g., Jerome S. Berg, "Judicial Interest in Administration: The Critical Variable," *Judicature* 57 (January 1974):251-55.

21. See, e.g., Neal Peirce, "Alabama's State Courts: A Model for the Nation," *Washington Post*, May 12, 1975, p. A-25.

22. Berg, "Judicial Interest."

23. Ibid., p. 253.

24. See, e.g., Saari, "Management and Courts."

25. Advisory Commission, *Report on State-Local Relations*, p. 195.

26. Interview with former state courts administrator, Tallahassee, Florida, February, 1975.

27. The assertion that a gradual process of change is most likely to succeed is becoming very popular. See, e.g., Larry Berkson and Steven W. Hays, "Injecting Court Administrators Into An Old System: A Case of Conflict in Florida," *Justice System Journal* 2 (Spring 1976):74-76.

28. Interviews with members of the Staff of the Joint Select Committee on Judicial Personnel of the Florida Legislature, Tallahassee, April 17, 1975. Resistance from deputy clerks may also be expected for other reasons. Traditional clerical processes have been vested with an element of "ceremony" that is favorably viewed by court employees. See William L. Whittaker, "Ceremony Versus Substance: Clerical Processes in the Courts," *Judicature* 56 (April 1973):374-76.

29. Governor Reubin Askew, as quoted in Joint Select Committee on Judicial Personnel of the Florida Legislature, "Transcript of Staff Report," unpublished paper, Tallahassee, January 13, 1975, p. 13.

30. Vassar B. Carlton as quoted in Staff of the Joint Select Committee on Judicial Personnel of the Florida Legislature, "Position Paper on the Implementation of Article V," unpublished paper, Tallahassee, November 1, 1973, p. 6.

31. Staff of the Joint Select Committee on Judicial Personnel of the Florida Legislature, "Discussion Concerning the Proposed Personnel Program," unpublished paper, Tallahassee, 1974, p. 3.

32. Ibid.

33. Ibid.

34. See Geoffrey C. Hazard, Jr., Martin B. McNamera, and Irwin F. Sentilles, III, "Court Finance and Unitary Budgeting," *Yale Law Journal* 81 (June 1972):1295-1300.

35. Harry O. Lawson, "Overview of Court Administration: A Commentary," paper prepared for delivery at the Institute for Court Management, American University, Washington, D.C., 1974, p. 23.

36. Hazard et al., "Court Finance."

37. Ibid.

38. Article V, Section 16 of the Florida Constitution states that the duties of court clerks may be divided between two officers, "one serving as clerk of court and one serving as ex officio clerk of the board of county commissioners, auditor, recorder. . . ." Thus, recording functions are clearly grouped with county responsibilities.

39. Joint Select Committee, "Transcript of Staff Report," at 19.

40. Edward E. Pringle, "Fiscal Problems of a State Court System," paper prepared for delivery to the Conference of Chief Justices, Seattle, August 11, 1972, p. 8.

41. Ibid., p. 10.

42. Ibid., p. 11.

43. Ibid.

Chapter 6
Conclusion

1. Missouri recently created a "unified" court system similar to Florida's, yet failed to alter the court clerks' role in the judicial system. See Barbara Schulert and Bill Hoelzel, "Court Reform," *Judicature* 60 (January 1977):281-83.

2. See Lynn W. Jensen and Francis E. Dosal, "Circuit Clerks' Study," *State Court Journal* 1 (Summer 1977):17-21.

3. See, e.g., Carl Baar, *Separate But Subservient: Court Budgeting in the American States* (Lexington, Mass.: D.C. Heath, 1975); and Jerome S. Berg, "The District Courts of Massachusetts," *Judicature* 59 (February 1976):344-52.

4. See, e.g., Peter Drucker, *Management: Tasks; Responsibilities; and Practices* (New York: Harper & Row, 1974).

5. Advisory Commission on Intergovernmental Relations, *State-Local Relations in the Criminal Justice System* (Washington, D.C.: Government Printing Office, 1971), p. 48.

6. The distinction between state financing and unitary budgeting has been discussed chiefly by Carl Baar. See Carl Baar, "The Limited Trend Toward Court Financing and Unitary Budgeting in the States," in Larry C. Berkson, Steven W. Hays, and Susan J. Carbon (eds.), *Managing the State Courts* (St. Paul: West Publishing, 1977), pp. 269-80.

7. See Samuel D. Conti, "The Courts: Summary and Recommendations," *State Court Journal* 1 (Spring 1977):18-20.

8. Berg, "The District Courts," p. 349.

9. See, e.g., Richard L. Chapman and Frederic N. Cleaveland, "The Changing Character of the Public Service and the Administrator in the 1980's," in Joseph A. Uveges, Jr. (ed.), *The Dimensions of Public Administration* (Boston: Holbrook Press, 1975), p. 596.

10. Berg, "The District Courts," pp. 349-51.

11. See, e.g., Eliot Friedson and Buford Rhea, "Processes of Control in a Company of Equals," *Social Problems* 11 (Fall 1963):119-31.

12. National Advisory Commission on Criminal Justice Standards and Goals, *The Courts* (Washington, D.C.: Government Printing Office, 1973), p. 183.

13. Robert A. Shapiro and Rachel N. Doan, "A Profile of State Court Administrators," *Judicature* 60 (October 1976):122.

14. Tom C. Clark, "The Need for Judicial Reform," *Washington Law Review* 48 (1973):810.

Index

Index

Administrative Judges, 45

Adversary System, 95

Advisory Commission on Intergovernmental Relations, 110

Alabama, 7, 90, 97

American Bar Association, 2, 3

American Bar Association *Standards Relating to Court Organization,* 2, 5, 36-67, 40, 109

Arkansas, 93

Article V of the *Florida Constitution,* 8-12, 21-22, 29, 44, 56, 58, 103

Askew, Reubin, 103

Baar, Carl, 6, 87

Berg, Jerome, 4, 99

Berkson, Larry C., 66

Board of Law Examiners, 88, 89

Burger, Warren, 3

California, 82, 93, 97

Campbell, Angus, 17

Carlton, Vassar B., 103

Carrigan, Jim R., 88

Case Disposition Reporting System, 27, 85, 86

Case Weighting, 86

Chief Circuit Administrator, 82

Chief Circuit Clerk, 82

Chief Judges, 22-28; administrative ability, 52, 73-74; administrative authority, 70, 99-100; Article V, 27-28, 97; case disposition reporting, 27; duties, 22, 24, 71; elective status, 49-50; opposition to state control, 97-99; perceptions of court executive assistants, 40-42, 100; perceptions of deputy clerks, 60-61; personnel administration, 58, 90-91; political activities, 26, 97; requirements for office, 22; role perceptions, 26; rotation in office, 74; selection, 74, 111; tenure, 50-51

Civil Courts, 8

Clerical Procedures, 54, 55

Computer Application, 54, 84

Conard, Alfred C., 94

Concurrent Jurisdiction, 2

Contingency Theory, 15

Conti, Samuel D., 82

County Commission, 45, 47, 52, 53, 55

County Courts, 8

County Judges Courts, 8

Court Clerks, 28-36; appointment of, 78, 81; Article V, 33; budget influence, 53, 155; court executive assistants, 42-43; duties, 29, elective status, 4, 77-78; interactions with chief judges, 43, 51; lobbying, 101-102; objections to state controls, 65, 100-103; personnel administration, 58-59, 61; professionalism, 33-34; requirements for office, 29; role, 20, 28, 29, 33-34; splitting office, 76; "Staff Competitors for Leadership," 4; training, 34-35

Court Delay, 1, 3, 9, 53

Court Executive Assistants, 36-44; chief judges' perceptions of, 40-42, 100; court clerks' perceptions of, 79, 101-102; duties, 36-37, 61, 72; growth of profession, 36-37; judges' assistants, 6; judicial vs. nonjudicial functions, 80-81; occupational dilemmas, 39; role perceptions, 38; selection, 37, 111; "Staff Competitors for Leadership," 4. *See also* Court Unification

Court Management Seminars, 57

Court Reform: components of, 5-7; controversial nature of, 93; court reporters, 45; gradualism, 99, 101; progress of, 5-8; resistance to, 95-96. *See also* court unification

Courts: as formal organizations, 12-15; as bureaucratic enigmas, 3; decen-

About the Author

Steven W. Hays is chairman of the department of public administration, California State University, Dominguez Hills. A specialist in criminal justice administration and public administration, he received the Ph.D. from the University of Florida. He is coeditor of *Managing the State Courts* and has authored several articles on court administration. He has also served as an urban consultant to cities in the Los Angeles Basin.